Kingfisher
Science
Encyclopedia

General Editor: Catherine Headlam

1

ABACUS ● BOILING POINT

Kingfisher

KINGFISHER
an imprint of Larousse plc
Elsley House, 24–30 Great Titchfield Street
London W1P 7AD

First published by Kingfisher 1991
Reprinted 1993, 1995 (with revisions) (twice), 1997

British Library Cataloguing-in-Publication Data
A catalogue record for this book is available from the British Library

ISBN 1 85697 447 2

Typesetting: Tradespools Ltd, Frome,
Somerset
Printed in Spain

GENERAL EDITOR
Catherine Headlam

EDITORIAL DIRECTOR
Jim Miles

ASSISTANT EDITORS
Lee Simmons
Charlotte Evans

EDITORIAL ASSISTANT
Andrea Moran

CONSULTANTS
Professor Lawrence F. Lowery, University of California, Berkeley, USA
Alison Porter, Education Officer, Science Museum, London

EDUCATIONAL CONSULTANTS
Terry Cash, Coordinator of a team of advisory teachers in Essex
Robert Pressling, Maths Coordinator,
Hillsgrove Primary School, London

CONTRIBUTORS
Joan Angelbeck
Michael Chinery
John Clark
Neil Curtis
Gwen Edmonds
Andrew Fisher
William Gould
Ian Graham
William Hemsley
James Muirden
John Paton
Brian Ward
Wendy Wasels
Peter Way

DESIGN
Ralph Pitchford
Allan Hardcastle
Ross George
Judy Crammond

PICTURE RESEARCH
Tim Russell
Elaine Willis

PRODUCTION
Dawn Hickman

SAFETY CODE

Some science experiments can be dangerous. Ask an adult to help you with difficult hammering or cutting and any experiments that involve flames, hot liquids or chemicals. Do not forget to put out any flames and turn off the heat when you have finished. Good scientists avoid accidents.

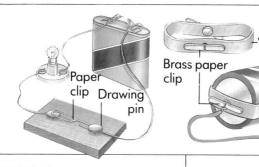

Paper clip

Drawing pin

Brass paper clip

Wide rubber band

ELECTRICITY
• Never use mains electricity for experiments.
• Use batteries for all experiments that need electricity. Dispose of batteries carefully when they are used up and never heat them up or take them apart.

HEATING
• Tie back hair and be careful of loose clothes.
• Only heat small quantities of a substance.
• Always have an adult with you.
• Never heat any container with a top on it. Always point what you are heating away from you.
• Never hold something in your hands to heat it. Use a holder that does not conduct heat.

SAFE SOURCES OF HEAT
• Hot water from the tap or kettle is a good source of heat.
• A hair dryer can be used to dry things. Always take care when using electricity near water.

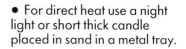

Sand

Metal tray

• For direct heat use a night light or short thick candle placed in sand in a metal tray.

CHEMICALS AND QUANTITIES
• Only use a small amount of any substance even if it is just salt or vinegar.
• Never taste or eat chemicals
• Clean up all spillages immediately, especially if on your skin.
• Wash your hands after using chemicals.
• Always ask an adult before using any substance; many cooking or cleaning substances used at home are quite powerful.
• Smell chemicals very carefully. Do not breathe in deeply any strong smells.
• Never handle chemicals with your bare hands. Use an old spoon and wash it very carefully after use.
• Label **all** chemicals.

SUN
• Never look directly at the Sun, especially when using a telescope or binoculars.

PLANTS AND ANIMALS
• Never pick wild flowers.
• Collect insects carefully so as not to harm them. Release them afterwards.
• Be careful of stinging insects.

SAFE CONTAINERS
• Use plastic containers if an experiment does not require heating or strong chemicals.
• Use heat-proof glass or metal containers if you are using heat.
• Avoid using ordinary glass as it may shatter.

CUTTING
• Use scissors rather than a knife whenever possible.
• When using a knife keep your fingers behind the cutting edge.
• Put what you are cutting on a board that will not slip and will prevent damage to the surface underneath.

ABOUT *your* ENCYCLOPEDIA

This encyclopedia is very easy to use. All the entries are arranged in alphabetical order. You should find most of the information you want by first looking up the main entry word. If the subject you are looking for does not have its own entry, look in the Index at the back. Usually you will find some information about your subject in another article.

•

Throughout the encyclopedia you will find words printed in small capitals, like this: LASER. These words are cross-references. When you see one, you will know that there is a separate entry on the subject in your encyclopedia. That entry may have more information about the subject you are looking up.

•

Subject symbols appear next to each heading. These will help you to relate each entry to one or more of the branches of science, such as Chemistry ◪ or Technology ◙. There are nine symbols in all.

•

Throughout the encyclopedia you will come across Special Feature entries. These take a large subject and look at it in more detail. Use them to help with a school project or to find out more about a particular branch of science. You will find a list of Special Features at the back of the encyclopedia.

•

In addition to the main text there are many See-For-Yourself panels with simple experiments for you to try. Use them to see-for-yourself how science works.

•

There are Fact Boxes and Milestones Boxes containing important facts and figures; Vocabulary Boxes which give the meaning of technical terms used in the main text; and Nugget Boxes which are full of fascinating and often surprising information.

•

Use your encyclopedia to discover a wealth of information about science, about how science works and about scientists and their discoveries.

•

HOW TO GET THE MOST
from your ENCYCLOPEDIA

This encyclopedia contains many features to help you look up things easily or simply to have fun just browsing through. Every page is illustrated and there are Fact Boxes, Special Feature entries, and literally hundreds of cross-references to help you find your way around. Some of these features are shown here. We hope you will get a lot of enjoyment from exploring your encyclopedia.

- Subject symbols
- Fact Boxes
- Nugget Boxes
- Special Feature entries
- Cross-references

- Simple experiments and observations
- Vocabulary Boxes
- Biography Boxes
- Milestones

BIOGRAPHY BOXES give details about the lives and work of individual scientists, and appear on the same page as the subject for which they are known.

THE TEXT is arranged alphabetically and easy to read. Cross-references appear as SMALL CAPITALS or *see also* suggestions. Turn to these entries for more information on the subject.

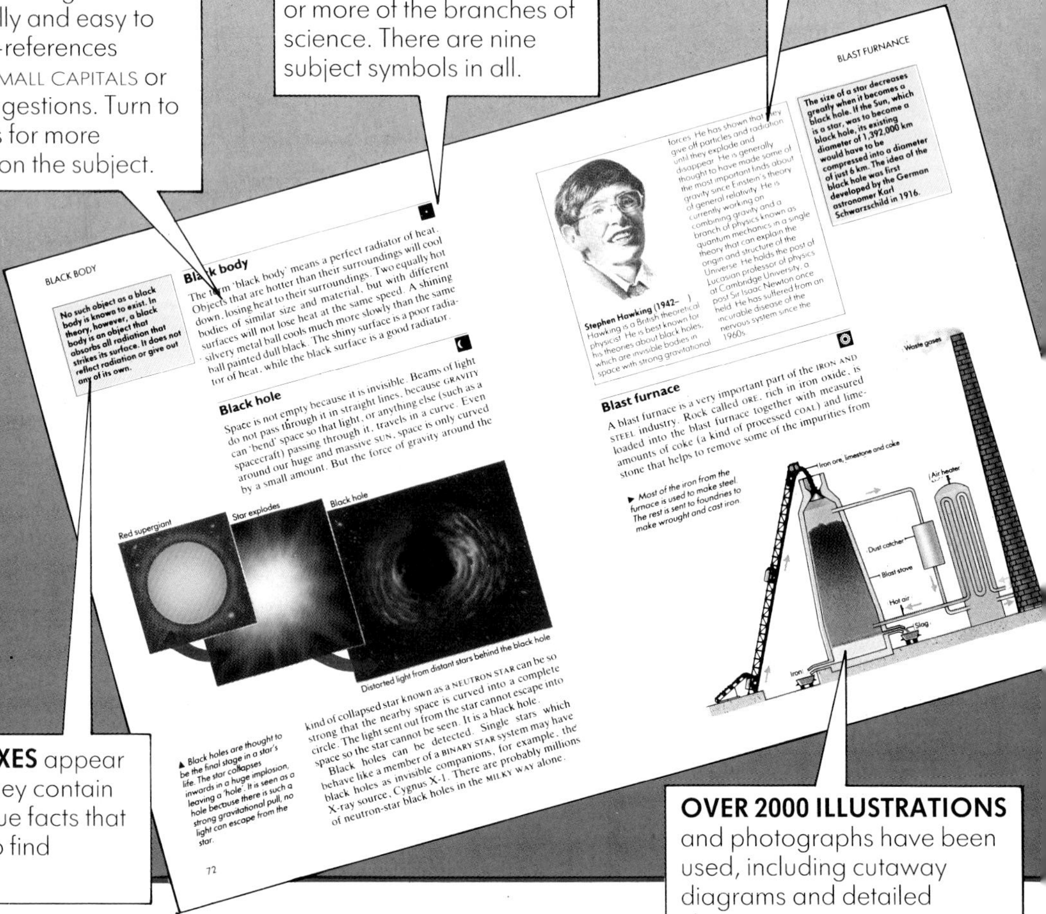

SUBJECT SYMBOLS allow you to relate an entry to one or more of the branches of science. There are nine subject symbols in all.

NUGGET BOXES appear throughout. They contain strange-but-true facts that you are sure to find fascinating.

OVER 2000 ILLUSTRATIONS and photographs have been used, including cutaway diagrams and detailed charts.

BLACK BODY

Black body

No such object as a black body is known to exist. In theory, however, a black body is an object that absorbs all radiation that strikes its surface. It does not reflect radiation or give out any of its own.

The term 'black body' means a perfect radiator of heat. Objects that are hotter than their surroundings will cool down, losing heat to their surroundings. Two equally hot bodies of similar size and material, but with different surfaces will not lose heat at the same speed. A shining silvery metal ball cools much more slowly than the same ball painted dull black. The shiny surface is a poor radiator of heat, while the black surface is a good radiator.

Black hole

Space is not empty because it is invisible. Beams of light do not pass through it in straight lines, because GRAVITY can 'bend' space so that light, or anything else (such as a spacecraft) passing through it, travels in a curve. Even around our huge and massive SUN, space is only curved by a small amount. But the force of gravity around the

Red supergiant | Star explodes | Black hole

Distorted light from distant stars behind the black hole

kind of collapsed star known as a NEUTRON STAR can be so strong that the nearby space is curved into a complete circle. The light sent out from the star cannot escape into space so the star cannot be seen. It is a black hole.

Black holes can be detected. Single stars which behave like a member of a BINARY STAR system may have black holes as invisible companions, for example, the X-ray source, Cygnus X-1. There are probably millions of neutron-star black holes in the MILKY WAY alone.

► Black holes are thought to be the final stage in a star's life. The star collapses inwards in a huge implosion, leaving a 'hole'. It is seen as a hole because there is such a strong gravitational pull, no light can escape from the star.

72

BLAST FURNACE

Stephen Hawking (1942–)
Hawking is a British theoretical physicist. He is best known for his theories about black holes, which are invisible bodies in space with strong gravitational forces. He has shown that they give off particles and radiation until they explode and disappear. He is generally thought to have made some of the most important finds about gravity since Einstein's theory of general relativity. He is currently working on combining gravity and a branch of physics known as quantum mechanics in a single theory that can explain the origin and structure of the Universe. He holds the post of Lucasian professor of physics at Cambridge University, a post Sir Isaac Newton once held. He has suffered from an incurable disease of the nervous system since the 1960s.

The size of a star decreases greatly when it becomes a black hole. If the Sun, which is a star, was to become a black hole, its existing diameter of 1,392,000 km would have to be compressed into a diameter of just 6 km. The idea of the black hole was first developed by the German astronomer Karl Schwarzschild in 1916.

Blast furnace

A blast furnace is a very important part of the IRON AND STEEL industry. Rock called ORE, rich in iron oxide, is loaded into the blast furnace together with measured amounts of coke (a kind of processed COAL) and limestone that helps to remove some of the impurities from

► Most of the iron from the furnace is used to make steel. The rest is sent to foundries to make wrought and cast iron

Waste gases

Iron ore, limestone and coke

Air heater

Dust catcher

Blast stove

Hot air

Slag

Iron

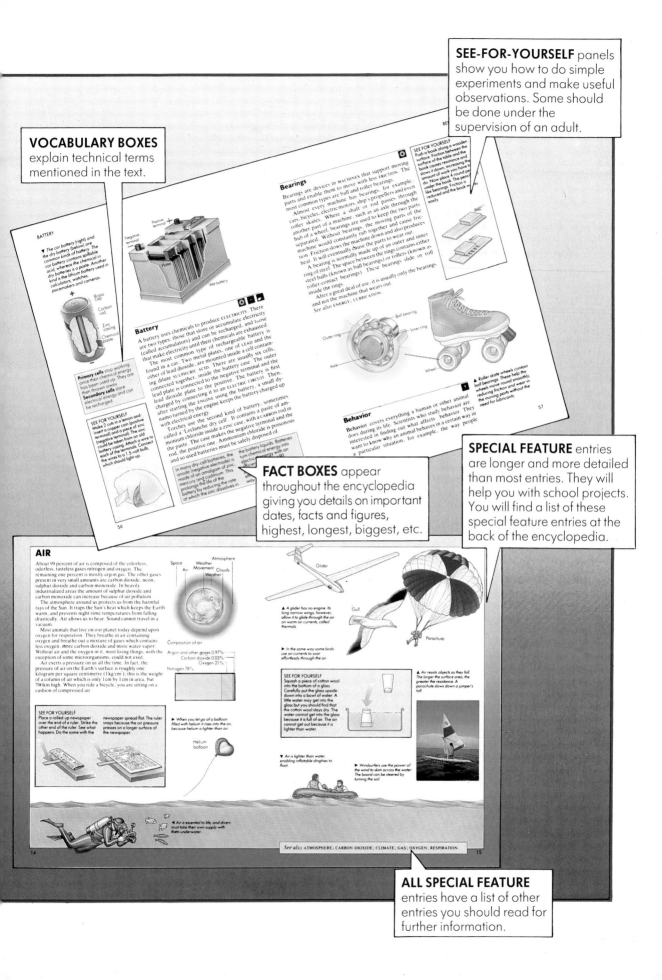

SEE-FOR-YOURSELF panels show you how to do simple experiments and make useful observations. Some should be done under the supervision of an adult.

VOCABULARY BOXES explain technical terms mentioned in the text.

FACT BOXES appear throughout the encyclopedia giving you details on important dates, facts and figures, highest, longest, biggest, etc.

SPECIAL FEATURE entries are longer and more detailed than most entries. They will help you with school projects. You will find a list of these special feature entries at the back of the encyclopedia.

ALL SPECIAL FEATURE entries have a list of other entries you should read for further information.

Bearings

Bearings are devices in MACHINES that support moving parts and enable them to move with less FRICTION. The most common types are ball and roller bearings. Almost every machine has bearings – for example, cars, bicycles, electric motors, ship's propellers and even roller skates. Where a shaft or rod passes through another part of a machine – such as an axle through the hub of a wheel, bearings are used to keep the two parts separated. Without bearings, the moving parts of the machine would constantly rub together and cause friction. Friction slows the machine down and also produces heat. It will eventually cause the parts to wear out.

A bearing is normally made up of an outer and inner ring of steel. The space between the rings contains either steel balls (known as ball bearings) or rollers (known as roller-contact bearings). These bearings slide or roll inside the rings.

After a great deal of use, it is usually only the bearings and not the machine that wears out.
See also ENERGY; LUBRICATION.

SEE FOR YOURSELF
Push a book along a wooden surface. Friction between the surface of the table and the book causes resistance and slows it down, increasing the amount of work you have to do. Now place 4 round pencils under the book. The pencils like bearings. Friction is reduced and the book moves easily.

Ball bearing — *Inner ring*
Outer ring
Axle — *Wheel*

▲ Roller skate wheels contain ball bearings. These help the wheels move round smoothly, reducing friction and wear in the moving parts without the need for lubricants.

57

BATTERY

▼ The car battery (right) and the dry battery (below) are common kinds of battery. The car battery contains spillable acid, whereas the chemical in dry batteries is a paste. Another kind is the lithium battery used in calculators, watches, pacemakers and cameras.

Positive terminal
Negative terminal
Plates
Wet battery

Brass cap
Carbon rod
Zinc casing
Chemical paste

Primary cells stop working once their chemical energy has been used up. They are then thrown away.
Secondary cells store electrical energy and can be recharged.

Battery

A battery uses chemicals to produce ELECTRICITY. There are two types: those that store or accumulate electricity (called accumulators) and can be recharged, and those that make electricity until their chemicals are exhausted.

The most common type of rechargeable battery is found in a car. Two metal plates, one of LEAD and the other of lead dioxide, are mounted inside a cell containing dilute SULPHURIC ACID. There are usually six cells connected together, inside the battery case. The outer lead plate is connected to the negative terminal and the lead dioxide plate to the positive. The battery is first charged by connecting it to an ELECTRIC CIRCUIT. Then, after starting the ENGINE using the battery, a small dynamo turned by the engine keeps the battery charged up with electrical energy.

Torches use the second kind of battery, sometimes called a 'Leclanche dry cell'. It contains a paste of ammonium chloride inside a ZINC case, with a CARBON rod in the paste. The case makes the negative terminal and the rod, the positive one. Ammonium chloride is poisonous and so used batteries must be safely disposed of.

SEE FOR YOURSELF
Make 2 cuts in a lemon and insert a copper coin (positive terminal) and a piece of zinc (negative terminal). The zinc could be taken from an old battery casing. Attach a wire to each of the terminals. Connect the wires to a 1.5-volt bulb, which should light-up.

In many dry-cell batteries, the anode (negative electrode) is made of an amalgam of zinc, mercury and cadmium. This prolongs the life of the battery by reducing the rate at which the zinc dissolves in [...] the battery liquids. Batteries turn chemical energy into electrical energy with an [...]

56

AIR

About 99 percent of air is composed of the colorless, odorless, tasteless gases nitrogen and oxygen. The remaining one percent is mostly argon gas. The other gases present in very small amounts are carbon dioxide, neon, sulphur dioxide and carbon monoxide. In heavily industrialized areas the amount of sulphur dioxide and carbon monoxide can increase because of air pollution.

The atmosphere acts as a protects us from the harmful rays of the Sun. It traps the Sun's heat which keeps the Earth warm, and prevents night-time temperatures from falling drastically. Air allows us to hear. Sound cannot travel in a vacuum.

Most animals that live on our planet today depend upon oxygen for respiration. They breathe in air containing oxygen and breathe out a mixture of gases which contains less oxygen, more carbon dioxide and more water vapor. Without air and the oxygen in it, most living things, with the exception of some microorganisms, could not exist.

Air exerts a pressure on us all the time. In fact, the pressure of air on the Earth's surface is roughly one kilogram per square centimetre (1 kg/cm²); this is the weight of a column of air which is only 1 cm by 1 cm in area, but 70 km high. When you ride a bicycle, you are sitting on a cushion of compressed air.

Space — *Air* — *Weather Movement* — *Atmosphere* — *Clouds* — *Weather*

Composition of air
Argon and other gases 0.97%
Carbon dioxide 0.03%
Oxygen 21%
Nitrogen 78%

▲ A glider has no engine. Its long narrow wings, however, allow it to glide through the air on warm air currents, called thermals.

► In the same way some birds use air currents to soar effortlessly through the air.

Glider
Gull
Parachute

▲ Air resists objects as they fall. The larger the surface area, the greater the resistance. A parachute slows down a jumper's fall.

SEE FOR YOURSELF
Place a rolled-up newspaper over the end of a ruler. Strike the other end of the ruler. See what happens. Do the same with the newspaper spread flat. The ruler snaps because the air pressure presses on a larger surface of the newspaper.

► When you let go of a balloon filled with helium it rises into the air, because helium is lighter than air.

Helium balloon

SEE FOR YOURSELF
Squash a piece of cotton wool into the bottom of a glass. Carefully put the glass upside-down into a bowl of water. A little water may get into the glass but you should find that the cotton wool stays dry. The water cannot get into the glass because it is full of air. The air cannot get out because it is lighter than water.

▼ Air is lighter than water, enabling inflatable dinghies to float.

► Windsurfers use the power of the wind to skim across the water. The board can be steered by turning the sail.

◄ Air is essential to life, and divers must take their own supply with them underwater.

14

See also ATMOSPHERE; CARBON DIOXIDE; CLIMATE; GAS; OXYGEN; RESPIRATION.

15

THE SUBJECT SYMBOLS

Each entry in this encyclopedia has its own easily recognized symbol opposite the heading. This symbol tells you at a glance which area of interest the entry falls into – is it Biography, Electronics, or Astronomy? Some entries fall into more than one subject area such as biochemistry which covers both Life Sciences and Chemistry. These entries have more than one subject symbol. Below are the nine subject areas we have used. At the back of the encyclopedia there is a list of all the articles divided into these subject areas.

ASTRONOMY
What are black holes, comets and quasars? How did planets and galaxies form? How much of space have we discovered and explored?

BIOGRAPHY
The lives and discoveries of important scientists and inventors and their contribution to current knowledge.

CHEMISTRY
What are substances made of? How do they behave on their own or when in contact with other substances?

EARTH SCIENCES
How the Earth was formed and how it is still changing; its deserts, mountains, oceans, rivers and weather.

ELECTRONICS
Explanations of devices based on controlling electrons, such as televisions and computers; how they work and how they are used.

LIFE SCIENCES
The structure and behaviour of living things; from microorganisms to the most complex plants and animals.

MATHEMATICS
How scientists use numbers and equations to analyse their experiments and to solve theoretical problems.

PHYSICS
Energy in the form of heat, light, sound, electricity, mechanics and magnetism, and the effect it has on matter from atoms to whole planets.

TECHNOLOGY
From simple adhesives to jet engines; how science is used in industry and the home.

Abacus √

An abacus is a counting device used by ancient Greeks and Romans, and some modern Eastern traders, in which rows of beads represent NUMBERS. Arithmetic calculations are made by sliding tne beads along wires or rods. Each row of beads has a different value. Different kinds of abacuses use different number systems. The five-bead abacus counts in ones, tens and hundreds on the left, and five times these on the right. When four beads have been slid to the right, they are returned to the left and one bead is moved on the right to represent five.

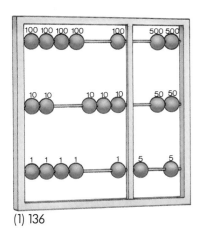

(1) 136

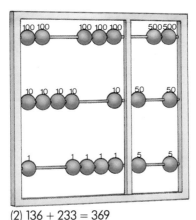

(2) 136 + 233 = 369

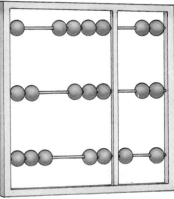

(3) 369 + ? = ?

▲ *Can you work out the missing numbers? Answer on page 3.*

Abrasives ⚙

When you rub sandpaper on a piece of wood to smooth it, you are using an abrasive. The tiny bits of sand in the sandpaper wear away the softer surface of the wood. Abrasives are used to smooth, grind, polish, sharpen, or cut other materials. Sand is the oldest abrasive. It was used to polish stone weapons and tools as early as 25,000 BC. Quartz and pumice are abrasives that are found in the earth. Carborundum is made from a mixture of powdered coke and clay heated in a furnace. It is very hard and can be used to polish gemstones.

Abrasives are also used in homes. Scouring powders and creams are used to clean pans and baths. Even toothpaste is a mild abrasive. It often contains finely powdered chalk.
See also HARDNESS.

▲ *Sand blasters blow quartz sand against stone walls to clean away dirt.*

Absolute zero *See* Kelvin

▼ The funny sinking feeling in your stomach when going down a big dipper is caused by the delay of your body in catching up with the acceleration and change in direction of the car.

Absorption

We generally use the word absorption to mean the soaking up of a LIQUID. Paper towels and sponges absorb liquids. In science, the word absorption is used in different ways. The roots of plants absorb water and other small MOLECULES from the soil. Animals' digestive systems break down food into simpler substances. These smaller molecules pass through the intestine walls and are absorbed into the BLOOD.

HEAT, LIGHT and SOUND are absorbed too. Dark objects absorb more heat than pale objects. People in hot countries paint their houses in light colours so they will absorb less heat. The heat is reflected off the outside of the house and the people stay cool inside.
See also ACOUSTICS; DIGESTION; REFLECTION.

Acceleration

When an object accelerates, its speed increases. If the driver of a car presses down the accelerator pedal and increases the speed, we say that the car is accelerating. The faster the speed increases, the greater the acceleration. An object can only accelerate if a FORCE 'pushes' or 'pulls' it. When a rifle is fired, the bullet accelerates along the barrel, pushed by the exploding gases. Once it leaves the barrel it begins to slow down (*decelerate*). This is because the air holds it back and GRAVITY pulls it towards the ground.

If you drop a ball from the top of a building, it accelerates as it falls. This is because it is being pulled down by gravity. The surprising thing about gravity is that it pulls

Acid gases from car exhausts and factories

everything down with the same FORCE, no matter how heavy it is. It produces a constant acceleration of 9.8 metres per second per second (m/s^2). After one second the ball would be travelling at a speed of 9.8 m/s, and after two seconds its speed would be 19.6 m/s, and so on. Only AIR resistance slows it down as it falls. If there was no air resistance, a feather would fall as fast as a cricket ball.

You can feel the effect of acceleration slightly in a lift. It is a problem for astronauts, who have to undergo very high acceleration levels in the first few seconds of take-off. If the spacecraft accelerates too fast, the force can make the astronauts feel ill and they may pass out.

See also MOVEMENT AND MOTION; VELOCITY.

Accumulator *See Battery*

Acid rain

Acid rain is caused by rain reacting with ACID gases, especially sulphur dioxide. These acid gases are waste GASES produced by factories, power stations and cars. The waste gases rise into the air and react with the rain water. Rain is normally slightly acid but this reaction makes it even more acid. This rain is what is known as 'acid rain'.

The WIND can carry the acid gases for long distances. Animal and plant life are threatened by acid rain as the rain slowly accumulates and increases the acidity of water in lakes, rivers and soil. Acid gases in the air cause damage even when it is not raining. Attempts are being made to reduce the amount of waste gases released.

See also POLLUTION; PRECIPITATION.

▲ *This tree shows the damaging effect acid rain is having on some woodlands throughout the world.*

Answers to Abacus question on page 1:
The number shown by the abacus is 437—four 100s, three 10s, one 5 and two 1s—and 68 has been added to 369.

▼ *Waste gases pollute the environment. They are carried in the air and fall to the ground, often far from their source, causing damage to aquatic life, trees and other vegetation.*

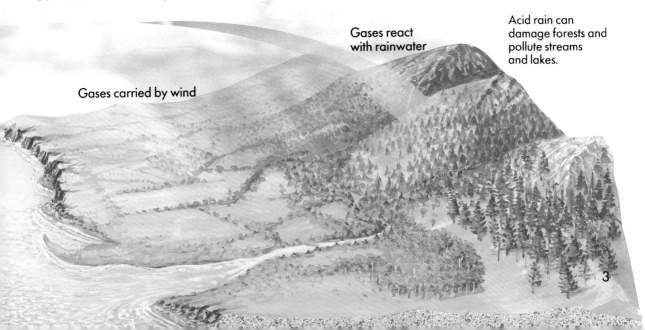

Gases react with rainwater

Acid rain can damage forests and pollute streams and lakes.

Gases carried by wind

3

Corrosive
chemicals

Bee

Fruits

▲ *The international warning symbol is found on vehicles carrying corrosive liquids. The bee's sting is acid and can hurt, but the acid in fruit is fairly harmless.*

SEE FOR YOURSELF
To see how an acid reacts, put a tablespoon of bicarbonate of soda onto the centre of a dish. Pour some vinegar (acid) onto the bicarbonate of soda. It starts to fizz as carbon dioxide is given off. The acid reacts with the bicarbonate to produce carbon dioxide.

Acids and Bases

The word 'acid' comes from the Latin word *acidus*, which means 'sour'; most acids have a sour taste. Some acids are poisons, some can cause serious skin burns, and others are quite harmless. Yet others are good to eat. We get citric acid from oranges and lemons. Our own bodies make acids to help us to digest our food.

One of the strongest and most important acids is SUL-PHURIC ACID. It is used in enormous quantities in the manufacture of fertilizers, petroleum products, and iron and steel. The liquid in car batteries is dilute (watered down) sulphuric acid. Other strong acids are NITRIC ACID and HYDROCHLORIC ACID.

Bases are substances that are the opposite of acids although, like acids, some bases are very reactive and corrosive such as lime (CALCIUM hydroxide) and CAUSTIC SODA. They are used in industrial processes. Magnesium hydroxide (the white powder or liquid we take to cure an upset acid STOMACH) is an example of a mild base. A base that can dissolve in water is called an alkali.

When an acid and a base are mixed in the right quantities, they neutralize each other (cancel each other out). For example, when hydrochloric acid is mixed with caustic soda the result is common salt and water.

Some substances change colour when they are put into an acid or base. These substances are called INDICATORS: LITMUS turns from blue to red in an acid solution and from red to blue in an alkaline solution.
See also CORROSION; pH.

Acoustics

The study of SOUND and how it travels is called acoustics. Sound waves travel in straight lines. Like LIGHT waves, they are absorbed or reflected by any objects that they may strike.

In a large room, sound waves are reflected back and forth from the walls and ceiling. Reflected sounds are ECHOES of the original sound. They may last for a few seconds before dying away completely. The sound waves that go directly to the listener are heard first, followed by sound reflected from around the room. Sound waves that bounce around are called reverberations. Good quality sound needs a little reverberation. More is needed for orchestral music, but not so much for

◄ An anechoic chamber (left) is used to test the acoustics of a vehicle so that the noise it produces can be reduced. The panels in the walls and ceiling of the room absorb the sound which is monitored (above).

speech. An architect must pay careful attention to acoustics when the inside of a concert hall or theatre is designed. The sound can be absorbed by the walls, the ceiling, the seating and even the people. The architect must calculate whether a clear sound will reach every seat. There must not be too much REFLECTION or ABSORPTION of the sound.

The larger a hall is, the more difficult it is to make the acoustics equally good for all the audience. In many halls, sound reflectors hung from the ceiling help to spread the sound evenly.

The number of people in a hall can affect the acoustics. People are quite good absorbers of sound, especially in winter when they are wearing a lot of clothes.

There are two major fields in the study of acoustics: **Architectural acoustics** provides the right conditions for listening to speech and music; **Environmental acoustics** deals with the control of noise pollution. Other areas of acoustic study: design of stereo equipment and telephones; measurement and protection of hearing; use of sound in making measurements and in processing materials.

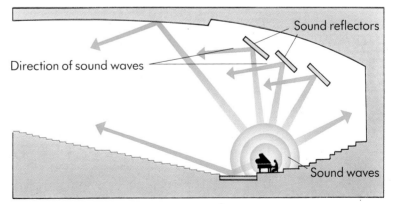

Sound reflectors

Direction of sound waves

Sound waves

▲ Halls are designed so that the sound waves can travel to everyone in the audience and clear sounds can be heard.

▲ Sounds made by an orchestra or a loudspeaker bounce off the walls, floors and ceiling. Ceilings in concert halls

must be hard and low to ensure good sound quality. Sound panels reflect sound down onto the audience.

Kestrel

Puffin

Curlew

Adaptation

An adaptation is a change in an organism, or object, to suit a new use or set of conditions. It could be a change in the set of characteristics of an animal or plant that helps it survive in its ENVIRONMENT. For example, polar bears have thick fur coats and a layer of fat under their skin. Both these characteristics are adaptations to their life in the cold arctic CLIMATE. Cacti live in DESERTS and are adapted to surviving without water for very long periods.

No two living things are born exactly the same, even identical twins have some differences. Often the differences are not important, but sometimes they can be important. This difference may improve the animal's chance of survival. It may live longer and have more offspring. After many generations, only individuals of that species with the useful variation are left. For example, giraffes with the longest necks will be able to reach and eat leaves from the highest branches. In a drought, when food is in short supply, giraffes with longer necks will be able to get more to eat than other giraffes and may be the only ones to survive and produce young. This is sometimes called 'survival of the fittest' which is part of NATURAL SELECTION, first suggested by the naturalist Charles DARWIN. He noted that birds' beaks are different shapes so that they can eat different kinds of food. These changes occurred over a very long period of time by small adaptations.

See also EVOLUTION; GENETICS; LAMARCK.

◀ Birds' bills suit their feeding habits. Birds of prey, such as the kestrel, have hooked bills to tear the flesh of prey. The saw-edged bill of the puffin enables it to carry several fish at once. Wading birds, like the curlew, have long, slender bills to dig deep into the mud. A hummingbird's long bill and tongue allows it to reach nectar deep inside a flower.

▶ Eskimos (Inuit) have adapted physically to the Arctic climate they live in. They have narrow eyes with folded eyelids to protect their eyes against the cold and a thick layer of flesh on their bodies for insulation.

Hummingbird

Adhesives

Adhesives are used to stick objects together. They can be made from natural materials such as bones, horns and animal skin which can be boiled to make glue. Plants with a lot of STARCH, such as potatoes, can also be used to make glue. Liquid rubber is another example of a good natural adhesive or glue.

Adhesives can also be made artificially (called synthetic adhesives). Synthetic adhesives are stronger than natural ones. Some, called *thermoplastics*, get soft when heated and hard again when cold. For example, synthetic resins (one kind of thermoplastic adhesive) are used to stick together the layers of glass that make the

safety glass of car windscreens. Other *thermosetting* adhesives become very hard when heated. They are usually made by mixing two chemicals and heating the mixture to make a very strong bond. Some thermosetting adhesives are used to stick the layers of plywood together. Among the strongest adhesives of all are EPOXY RESINS. *See also* PLASTICS.

SEE FOR YOURSELF
Make your own adhesive. Warm half a litre of skimmed milk, and add 2 tablespoons of vinegar stirring all the time. A white lumpy substance, casein, will form. Strain off the lumps of casein and mix them with 2 tablespoons of warm water and 6 tablespoons of bicarbonate of soda. Mash and force the mixture through a sieve. Leave it to stand in a pot for a day before using.

◄ *This commercial adhesive is undergoing a bond strength test. The bonded surfaces are being forced apart and the adhesive is resisting. Surfaces must be absolutely clean for a successful bond.*

Superglues are capable of bonding all types of surfaces within seconds. Every care should be taken when handling such adhesives as they are extremely dangerous if they come into contact with the skin or eyes.

Adolescence

Adolescence is the time in our lives when we are no longer children, and yet we are not fully grown up. The length of adolescence varies because everyone is different, but it usually begins earlier in girls. It may start as early as 9 years and end as late as 24 years.

When a child reaches adolescence his or her body will begin to change in a number of ways. Both boys and girls will develop hair under their arms and between their legs. A boy will develop a deeper voice and a beard will start to grow. A girl's breasts will start to develop and her hips will widen. Also, a girl will start to have the monthly menstrual periods which mean that one day she will be able to have children.

Confused emotions are common during adolescence, not only because of HORMONE changes, but also because adolescents begin to depend less on their parents.

▼ Boys and girls grow rapidly during adolescence. However, the rate differs between the sexes. Girls tend to gain weight and height about the age of 12 years, whereas boys tend to develop later, usually between 16 and 18 years.

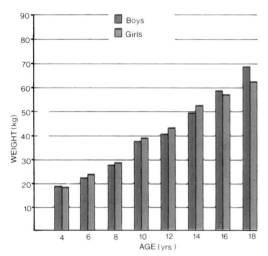

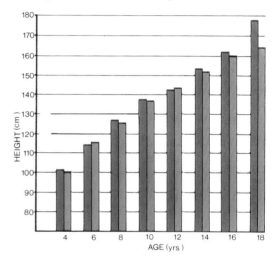

Aerial *See* Antenna

Aerodynamics

Aerodynamics is the science that deals with AIR moving against an object, like wind filling the sails of a boat; or something moving through the air, like an aircraft flying through the sky.

How does a kite fly? How does a glider soar through the air with no ENGINE? How does a jumbo jet weighing more than 350,000 kg stay in the air? The answers to these questions come from aerodynamics.

The top surface of an aircraft's wing is curved, while the bottom is flatter. This shape is called an *aerofoil*. As the plane cuts through the air, the air that flows over the top of the wing has to travel a greater distance than the air flowing underneath the wing, so it has to travel faster over the top. It is a scientific law, called Bernoulli's Principle, that air PRESSURE (or the pressure of a liquid)

SEE FOR YOURSELF
Blow steadily over the top of a strip of paper. Your breath reduces the pushing power of the air above the paper. The stronger air pressure underneath lifts it up.

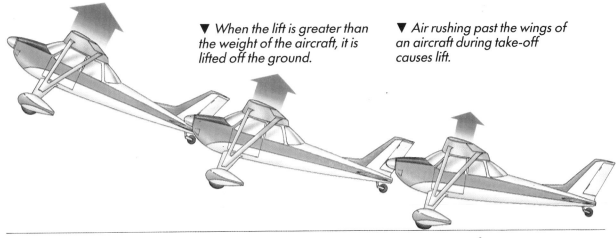

▼ *When the lift is greater than the weight of the aircraft, it is lifted off the ground.*

▼ *Air rushing past the wings of an aircraft during take-off causes lift.*

decreases when the flow of air (or liquid) speeds up. Because there is less pressure on the top surface of an aircraft's wing than on the bottom, the wing is pushed upwards. This upward force is called *lift*, and the lift is greater the faster the aircraft flies.

But the aircraft is also held back by the resistance of the air. This resistance is called *drag*. The faster an aircraft flies, the more drag there is. Drag is a particular problem in designing high-speed planes because drag increases much faster than the speed of the plane. To reduce drag, all parts of the plane that are in contact with the air are STREAMLINED. Streamlining helps the air to flow smoothly over the plane.

Planes, cars, and trains are all designed with smooth,

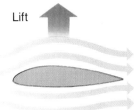

Lift

Wing shape: low drag

▲ *The aerodynamic shape of an aircraft's wing is important in reducing drag.*

Air flow

Eddies

Round shape: medium drag

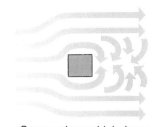

Square shape: high drag

▲ *Angles or sharp curves on objects break up the airflow and cause eddies, or swirls of air, increasing drag.*

◄ *Wind tunnels are used to test new car designs. A car with a streamlined shape will go faster and use less fuel because it has low drag.*

9

▲ *Modern trucks have specially designed cab roofs that direct the airflow up and over the load behind.*

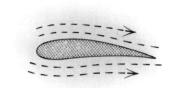

Daniel Bernoulli (1700–1782)
Bernoulli was a Swiss doctor and mathematician. He showed that when the speed of a liquid increases, the pressure of the liquid drops. In the same way air, flows faster over the curved upper surface of an aircraft wing than the air passing under the flatter lower surface. This means that the air pressure below the wing is greater than the pressure above, which creates an upward lift.

curved bodies to reduce drag. When they are being designed, models are tested in WIND TUNNELS where an airstream is blown over the model by a fan. If smoke is put into the wind tunnel, the designers can see how the air flows around the model. By making adjustments, the most efficient aerodynamic shape can be found.

Aeroplane *See* Flight

Aerosol

An aerosol is a cloud of fine particles suspended in a GAS. The particles can be liquid, or solid as in smoke.

The term aerosol is often applied to the can that produces this spray. Aerosols are used to spray such products as paints and cosmetics. The contents of the can consist of the product to be sprayed and a liquefied gas under PRESSURE. The gas is called a propellant because it propels the product out of the can. When the button on the top of the can is pressed, a valve is opened and the product is forced out as a spray. The spray consists of the vaporized gas with the product suspended in it. An atomizer works by producing a fine spray of liquid particles without using a pressurized propellant.

Common propellants are CHLOROFLUOROCARBONS or CFCs. Over the years research has shown that CFCs are helping to create a hole in the OZONE LAYER. Steps are now being taken to replace CFCs with less damaging propellants with less chlorine and fluorine in them.

Button released and valve closed

Button pressed down and valve open

Valve

Button

Nozzle

Button

Aerosol spray

Pressure

Liquefied propellant and product

▲ *Pressing the button on an aerosol opens the valve. The pressure of the liquefied propellant forces the product up through the tube and out of the nozzle as a spray.*

Aging

As animals grow old, many changes take place in the way they function and in the way they look. Humans age more slowly than most other animals. People in the

◄ *Four generations are present in this family group. All are at different stages of the aging process.*

industrialized countries generally live to about 70 years, with women outliving men on average by a few years. In poorer countries people generally have shorter life-spans. In the animal kingdom, elephants live for up to 70 years, horses 40 years, dogs 20 years, and mice about 4 years. These seem to be maximum ages. Some birds have longer lifespans. Parrots and eagles, for instance, can live for over 100 years.

As people get older, their SKIN becomes wrinkled and their HAIR grey. Their MEMORY may become poor and their EYES, EARS, TASTE and sense of smell may deteriorate. But different people age at different rates. Two people 70 years old may be quite different in their strength and mental ability.

Over the last 100 years, doctors have become better at keeping people alive by curing and preventing disease. This means that there is an increasing number of old people in the population. But doctors still do not know what causes our bodies to wear out with the years.

Bristlecone pine

▲ *Trees are the longest living organisms on Earth. Bristlecone pines can live for up to 5000 years.*

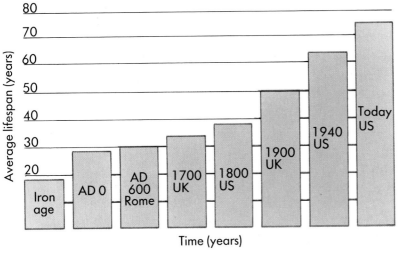

Average lifespan (years) / Time (years)

Iron age	AD 0	AD 600 Rome	1700 UK	1800 US	1900 UK	1940 US	Today US

Aging is not simply a process of cells dying. Most cells keep renewing themselves, although not all cells have the same average lifespan. For example, skin cells only survive 19 days, whereas red blood cells last 3 weeks and bone cells can live for 25 years or more.

◄ *Better living conditions and advances in medicine are responsible for the increase in life expectancy over the centuries.*

AGRICULTURE

Agriculture is the world's largest and most important industry. It probably began about 10,000 years ago. Today it produces over 95 percent of the world's food and provides us with many kinds of oil and fibre. Nearly half of the world's work-force is employed in agriculture, growing crops or looking after farm animals. Sheep and goats were the first animals to be domesticated, but cattle are now the most important farm animals. There are over 12 billion of them in the world, providing us with meat, milk and leather. In some countries, they are still used to pull carts and ploughs. Pigs and buffaloes are the other major farm animals.

Cereals were the first cultivated crops, but about 100 different kinds of plants are now grown for food. People soon invented simple ploughs pulled by animals, but agriculture changed very slowly until about 100 years ago. Since then there have been tremendous advances in plant and animal breeding and in the use of fertilizers and pesticides, which have led to better crops. The great advances in engineering mean that today's farmers can use huge ploughs pulled by powerful tractors and all sorts of other machinery to help them harvest and move crops.

George Washington Carver (1864–1943)
Carver was an American educator and agricultural scientist. He worked to improve crop production and agricultural methods. He encouraged farmers of the Southern States to grow soil-enriching peanuts and sweet potatoes. He discovered many uses for the new crops. From peanuts he made over 300 products including soap and ink.

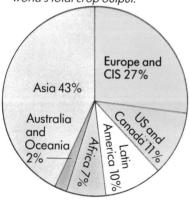

▼ About a third of the Earth's total land area is used for farming. About a third of this land is used to grow crops. The pie chart shows how world regions contribute to the world's total crop output.

Asia 43%
Europe and CIS 27%
US and Canada 11%
Latin America 10%
Africa 7%
Australia and Oceania 2%

▲ Because the environment within greenhouses can be controlled, they are useful for cultivating crops outside normal growing seasons.

◀ Some farming methods are slow and use much human and animal labour.

▶ The development of farm machinery means that several jobs can be done at once, speeding up production.

Brussels sprouts harvester

Plough

Oxen

See also BREEDING; CEREALS; FERTILIZERS; HORTICULTURE; HYDROPONICS; PESTICIDES.

AIDS

AIDS, Acquired Immune Deficiency Syndrome, is caused by a VIRUS named HIV. The AIDS virus attacks certain white blood cells that form an important part of the body's IMMUNE SYSTEM. This fights off viruses and bacteria when they enter the body. When these white blood cells are destroyed, the patient can become very ill with a disease which would not be serious in a healthy person. Because the body of a person with AIDS has lost its means of fighting disease, the patient can often die.

AIDS is passed from person to person in three main ways: by intimate sexual contact, by exposure to blood infected with HIV, and by transmission to a baby in an infected mother's womb. People most likely to catch AIDS are drug addicts who inject drugs into themselves and who share hypodermic needles. However, anyone can develop the disease through intimate sexual contact with somebody who has the HIV virus. People who have been infected with the HIV virus may not become seriously ill until years later.

AIDS was first identified in 1981. Since then it has become a serious problem throughout the world.

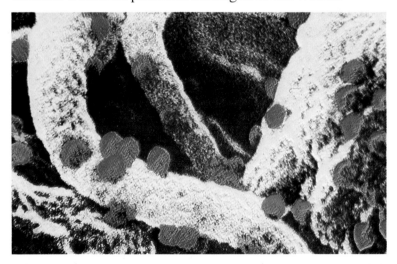

Air

Air is a mixture of GASES. The layer of air which surrounds the Earth is called the ATMOSPHERE. We cannot see or smell air, yet it is as real as the chair you are sitting on. Moving air can turn windmills, blow down large trees, and, if it is compressed, can break up solid concrete as in PNEUMATIC drills. *See* pages 14 and 15.

HIV Human Immunodeficiency Virus.
AIDS Acquired Immune Deficiency Syndrome.
Syndrome A combination of symptoms/signs showing that a condition/illness exists.

▼ When the AIDS virus enters a white blood cell, the core of the virus breaks open and releases its genetic material (DNA). The virus DNA takes over the white blood cell which begins to make copies of the virus and then dies.

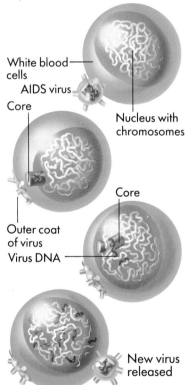

White blood cells
AIDS virus
Core
Nucleus with chromosomes
Outer coat of virus
Virus DNA
Core
New virus released

◄ The AIDS virus travels in the bloodstream. It gets inside certain white blood cells which fight off infection. The AIDS virus uses the white blood cell to produce many new viruses (**red**). These break out of the white blood cell and go on to infect more white blood cells, weakening the immune system.

AIR

About 99 percent of air is composed of the colourless, odourless, tasteless gases nitrogen and oxygen. The remaining one percent is mostly argon gas. The other gases present in very small amounts are carbon dioxide, neon, sulphur dioxide and carbon monoxide. In heavily industrialized areas the amount of sulphur dioxide and carbon monoxide can increase because of air pollution.

The atmosphere around us protects us from the harmful rays of the Sun. It traps the Sun's heat which keeps the Earth warm, and prevents night-time temperatures from falling drastically. Air allows us to hear. Sound cannot travel in a vacuum.

Most animals that live on our planet today depend upon oxygen for respiration. They breathe in air containing oxygen and breathe out a mixture of gases which contains less oxygen, more carbon dioxide and more water vapour. Without oxygen, most living things, with the exception of some microorganisms, could not exist.

Air exerts a pressure on us all the time. In fact, the pressure of air on the Earth's surface is roughly one kilogram per square centimetre ($1\,kg/cm^2$); this is the weight of a column of air which is only 1 cm by 1 cm in area, but 700 km high. When you ride a bicycle, you are sitting on a cushion of compressed air in the tyres.

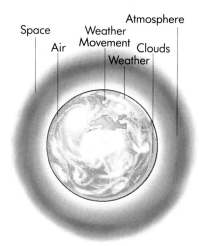

Composition of air

Argon and other gases 0.97%
Carbon dioxide 0.03%
Oxygen 21%
Nitrogen 78%

▲ The air (top) cloaks the Earth in a layer we call the atmosphere. The movement of air is responsible for our weather patterns. The chart, (above) shows the gases which make up air.

SEE FOR YOURSELF
Place a rolled-up newspaper over the end of a ruler. Strike the other end of the ruler. See what happens. Do the same with the newspaper spread flat. The ruler snaps because the air pressure presses on a larger surface of the newspaper.

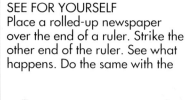

▶ When you let go of a balloon filled with helium it rises into the air, because helium is lighter than air.

Helium balloon

◀ Air is essential to life, and divers must take their own supply with them underwater.

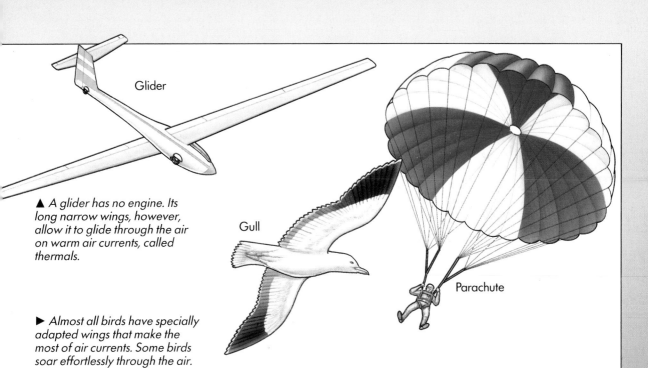

Glider

Gull

Parachute

▲ A glider has no engine. Its long narrow wings, however, allow it to glide through the air on warm air currents, called thermals.

▶ Almost all birds have specially adapted wings that make the most of air currents. Some birds soar effortlessly through the air.

SEE FOR YOURSELF
Squash a piece of cotton wool into the bottom of a glass. Carefully put the glass upside-down into a bowl of water. A little water may get into the glass but you should find that the cotton wool stays dry. The water cannot get into the glass because it is full of air. The air cannot get out because it is lighter than water.

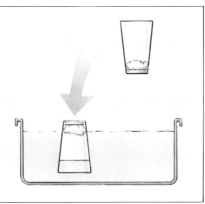

▲ Air resists objects as they fall. The larger the surface area, the greater the resistance. A parachute slows down a jumper's fall.

▼ Air is lighter than water, enabling inflatable dinghies to float.

▶ Windsurfers use the power of the wind to skim across the water. The board can be steered by turning the sail.

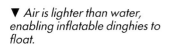

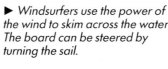

See also ATMOSPHERE; CARBON DIOXIDE; CLIMATE; GAS; OXYGEN; RESPIRATION.

The term air conditioning was first used in 1906 by Stuart Cramer, an American textile engineer. It was used to describe scientific systems that would clean, circulate and control the temperature and humidity of air inside buildings. People have, however, been devising methods of 'conditioning' the air for many hundreds of years. The ancient Egyptians hung wet mats inside their buildings through which the wind blew, evaporating the water and cooling the air.

Air conditioning

Air conditioning controls the moisture level, TEMPERATURE and movement of AIR inside buildings. Air conditioning is responsible for the great drop in temperature that you notice when you walk into some shops or stores on a hot day. Outside it is hot and sticky but inside it is quite cold. An air conditioning unit uses fans to draw in air from the outside of the building. The air is then passed over a refrigerated HEAT EXCHANGER. The ice-cold grills of the heat exchanger take in the heat from the air so that only cold air is blown through the wide channels built into the ceiling or walls. Air conditioning can heat up air as well as cooling it.

Air conditioning is not just available for large buildings, many homes in the United States have small units that fit into a single window pane. Units can be made small enough to fit inside cars, making travel in even the hottest countries pleasantly cool. Air conditioning is used in many places where manufacturing processes need to be run at a steady temperature. Even small temperature changes can affect the size of METAL components, so air conditioning is essential.

See also CONTRACTION; EXPANSION; REFRIGERATION.

▼ *This is a central air conditioning system as all the conditioned air comes from one source. The liquid refrigerant removes the heat from the air,* which is then blown through air ducts into the building. Used air is mixed with air from the outside, conditioned and then returned to the building. To heat the air, coils filled with hot water or steam are used. The air is warmed up as it passes over the coils before being blown round the building.

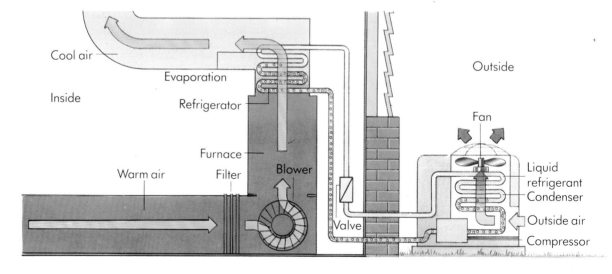

Air cushion vehicle *See* Hovercraft

Air pollution

Much of the AIR we breathe is polluted and occasionally it may smell unpleasant. Pollution can cause irritation of the nose and throat, and lengthy exposure to some types of pollution may cause serious disorders.

Most air pollution comes from BURNING fuels. We burn fuels in industrial processes, in motor vehicles, in heating our homes and in the production of ELECTRICITY (with the exception of nuclear power stations).

Smoke and SULPHUR DIOXIDE come from burning coal.

These can affect people's LUNGS, causing bronchitis and other illnesses. In 1952, from 5 to 9 December, 4000 people died from heart and lung failure in dense fog in London. It was caused by smoke and unusual weather conditions. After this disaster the government made the use of smokeless fuels, for example, anthracite (a kind of coal), compulsory in many parts of Britain.

The exhausts of motor vehicles release several harmful GASES and are a major cause of air pollution. They also put LEAD into the ATMOSPHERE. Lead has become a major pollutant in areas of heavy traffic, and lead-free petrol may eventually be the only kind available.

Cigarette smoke can pollute air at home and at work. Scientists have shown that cigarette smoke is not only damaging to the health of people who smoke but also, to a lesser degree, to the health of non-smokers who breathe other people's cigarette smoke.

So how can air pollution be controlled? Laws now insist that industries filter, destroy or dilute polluting substances before they are allowed to escape into the air. Eventually we will be free from this type of pollution.

◀ *The unhealthy yellow haze hanging over this city is called smog and is made up of large numbers of tiny particles of factory smoke, exhaust fumes and other pollutants.*

▼ *Carbon monoxide (CO) is pumped into the atmosphere by industry, as it burns fuel to provide energy for manufacturing processes. Carbon monoxide is the main pollutant in vehicle exhaust fumes. It can build up in dangerous amounts in crowded cities with heavy traffic.*

Sources of carbon monoxide pollution (% of total)

Industrial processes 6.8%

Fuel combustion 10.3%

Miscellaneous 12.3%

(including solid waste disposal, chemical spray)

Transportation 70.6%

Roger Bacon (1214–1292)
An English monk and alchemist, Bacon became known as the founder of experimental science. He believed that doing experiments for yourself was the way to learn about nature rather than just accepting what other people tell you. His most important work was the *Opus Maius*, in which he wrote about the scientific method of learning. He did many experiments. He showed how rainbows are made by the effect of water-drops on sunlight, and how lenses could be used to help people with weak sight.

Alchemy

Most of our modern ideas about CHEMISTRY, our knowledge of ATOMS, MOLECULES, ELEMENTS and COMPOUNDS and so on, date back only to about 1700. Before that time, the make-up of substances was a mystery. The people who tried to uncover the mystery were called alchemists and their field of study, alchemy.

Alchemy mixed magic with science, secret semi-religious rituals and philosophy. It was based on ancient Chinese, Indian and Greek theories about the natural world. In the Middle Ages, Arabs trading with China passed on knowledge of alchemy to Egypt and then into Europe, where many people studied it.

Some alchemists were cheats and tricksters, but others, such as Roger Bacon, were serious researchers who laid the foundations for chemistry and MEDICINE.

The alchemists believed in ARISTOTLE's view that everything in the UNIVERSE was made up of four elements, earth, air, water and fire. They believed that if they could change the balance of these elements, they could turn one substance into another and, particularly turn lead into gold. They tried without success. They also searched unsuccessfully for a medicine that would prolong human life, perhaps for ever. They did, however, discover ALCOHOL and many natural substances that could be used to make DRUGS.

► The Alchemist *painted by Joseph Wright in 1771 shows Hennig Brand, his face lit by the glow of his new discovery, phosphorus.*

Alcohol

Alcohols are members of a group of chemical compounds that contain atoms of CARBON, hydrogen and OXYGEN. All alcohols are liquids. We usually think of alcohol as an ingredient of beer, wine and spirits. But this is really only one of the many types of chemicals called alcohols, most of which are important in industry. The majority of alcohols are used as SOLVENTS (substances that dissolve other substances). Methanol, or wood alcohol, is very poisonous and is used for making plastics, paints and varnishes. Ethanol, or ethyl alcohol, is the alcohol present in alcoholic drinks. It is produced naturally by FERMENTATION, in which YEAST acts on sugar to make ethanol and carbon dioxide. Ethanol is used as an ingredient in flavourings, detergents and perfumes. It is also mixed with petrol to improve its OCTANE ('star') rating. Different alcohols are also used as solvents for sticky substances called resins, making cosmetics and lotions. Ethylene glycol, a poisonous alcohol, is an ingredient of ANTIFREEZE which prevents the coolant liquid in motor-vehicle engines from freezing.

The main types of alcohols are as follows:
Methanol is very toxic and is obtained from methane. There are two kinds of **Propanol**. One is a solvent used in the manufacture of some plastics and the other is used as a de-icer in liquid fuels and also as a solvent. **Ethylene glycol** is also toxic. It is used mainly as an antifreeze. **Plasticizer alcohols** are used to make plastics flexible. **Detergent alcohols** are used in soaps and detergents.

▼ *All these products contain an alcohol compound.*

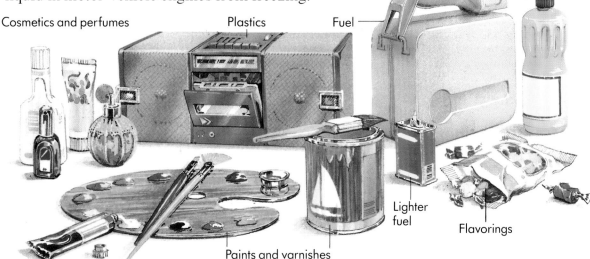

Cosmetics and perfumes — Plastics — Fuel — Detergents — Lighter fuel — Flavorings — Paints and varnishes

Algebra

Algebra is a branch of MATHEMATICS. It links together the other branches of mathematics into a single subject. Algebra was developed from its origins by the Arabs over a thousand years ago. In its simplest form, algebra is like ARITHMETIC but uses letters and symbols to stand for numbers. For example, we know that 2+5=7 and that 5+2=7. So we can say that 2+5=5+2. If you take any

The Persian poet Omar Khayyam, who lived in the 11th century and who wrote a famous poem called the *Rubaiyat*, spent most of his time in the study of algebra. His work on algebra was known throughout Europe, but no one seems to have admired his verses then.

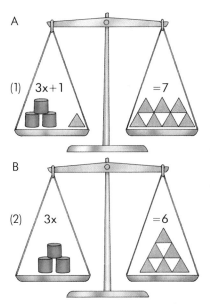

A

(1) $3x+1$ $=7$

B

(2) $3x$ $=6$

▲ Equations are like scales. The sides must always balance. Can you find the value of x, represented as a cylinder in the diagram? Answer on page 23.

Allergies can be caused by a variety of different substances. Dust, pollen spores, mould, animal hairs and cigarette smoke may cause respiratory allergies such as asthma, hay fever and an all-year-round nasal allergy known as perennial rhinitis. Certain foods may produce allergic reactions. Chocolate and cheese may be the cause of some allergic headaches, whereas cow's milk, gluten and shellfish may provoke digestive disorders, such as stomachache and sickness.

▶ Skin tests are used to find out which substance is causing an allergy. Small doses of common allergens are injected just below the skin. The skin will usually become red where the substances to which the person is allergic have been injected.

two numbers, you can add them together either way and get the same answer. To show that this is true for any pair of numbers, we can let a stand for one and b stand for the other. Then we can write, $a+b=b+a$. Another example is $a \times b = b \times a$ (or $ab=ba$, for short). Algebra can solve problems by employing letters to stand for unknown values.

Alkali *See* Acids and Bases

Allergy

An allergy is when your body reacts against a substance which is actually quite harmless. Allergies usually develop after you have been exposed to a substance several times. At first, the body tolerates the substance, but after a time, it becomes sensitive to it. Then every time you encounter this substance, called an ANTIGEN or allergen, the body tries to destroy it. It does this by releasing chemicals including histamines, which can cause an uncomfortable allergic reaction like hay fever. Drugs, called antihistamines, that prevent the production of histamines, are often used to treat allergies.

Hay fever is the most common form of allergy. It is caused by breathing in clouds of pollen which are released by grass and other plants during the spring and summer months. For most people, this does no harm at all, but for people who are sensitive to pollen, it causes symptoms similar to a streaming cold, with sneezing, and red watery eyes.

We can develop allergies to many different things and some people are allergic to foods such as strawberries or

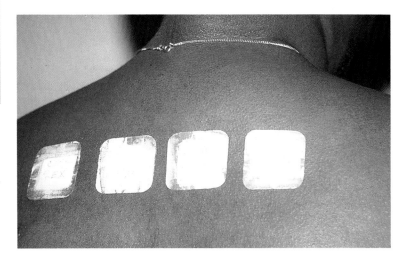

milk. Another form of allergy causes an irritating SKIN rash called dermatitis. This type of allergy is caused by the skin rubbing against a material which contains the antigen. For example, many people are allergic to the NICKEL plating on press studs, zip fasteners and buckles used on clothes.

Alloy

An alloy is a mixture of two or more METALS, and sometimes, also, a non-metal. They are most commonly produced by heating and melting the substances together. The first man-made alloy we know of was bronze (a mixture of COPPER and TIN), which was widely used to make items such as pots and pans, swords and spears, as long as 6000 years ago. Two other well-known alloys are brass (copper and ZINC) and steel (IRON and CARBON).

Today there are thousands of alloys, each produced for some special purpose. There are those that have high tensile strength (they can resist great WEIGHT or PRESSURE without breaking), those that can withstand very

▲ Bronze was often used to make tools, weapons, helmets and ornaments. The shield and dagger date from the 1st century BC; they were dredged up from the River Thames in London. The helmet is Greek and was made 500 BC.

◄ Special aluminium alloys have been developed for use in aircraft manufacturing, because aircraft parts must be strong and light.

high temperatures and those that have a strong resistance to acids or other forms of CORROSION. Other alloys conduct ELECTRICITY very easily, or are good insulators (they do not allow electricity to pass).
See also AMALGAM; CONDUCTION.

Alpha particles See Radioactivity

Alternating current See Electricity

Alternator See Generator

Bronze was so important in history that there is a period of history called the Bronze Age. This is because bronze is harder than copper on its own and therefore had many more uses.

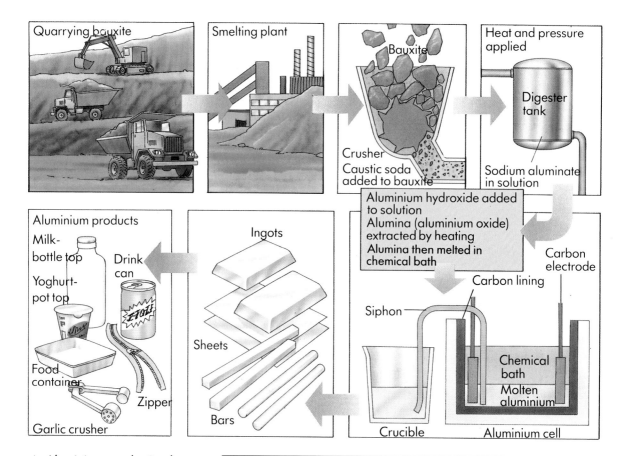

▲ *Aluminium production has two main stages. Alumina is extracted from bauxite and smelted to obtain aluminium.*

▼ *Drink cans are made from aluminium because it is light and does not corrode easily.*

Aluminium

Aluminium is a lightweight, silver-coloured metallic ELEMENT. It readily reacts with the oxygen in the air to form a surface coating of aluminium oxide called alumina. This coating preserves it from further CORROSION or wear. Aluminium is the commonest METAL in the Earth's crust, and a large number of things are made out of it, from saucepans, tinfoil and drink cans to tanks and the fuselage of aircraft.

Although it is common, aluminium is difficult and costly to get at because it only occurs in COMPOUNDS and never as pure aluminium. It is extracted from a mineral called bauxite using electrical power.

Aluminium can be easily bent, it can be hammered into different shapes, and drawn out into thin wires. It is a good conductor of electricity and can be mixed with other metals to form very strong ALLOYS. Aluminium is present in plants such as tea, and is used in drugs such as aspirin. Many doctors fear that too much aluminium can affect the brain and may cause illness in old people and new-born babies.

Amalgam

An amalgam is a special form of ALLOY. It is a mixture of METALS, in which one of the metals is MERCURY. Mercury is a most unusual metal because it is a liquid, bright silver in colour and very heavy. Most common metals, apart from iron and platinum, can be combined with mercury to form amalgams. Amalgams have many uses. Silver/mercury amalgams are sometimes used in dentistry for fillings. Mercury/tin amalgams were once used to coat the backs of mirror glasses.

Mercury is used in the extraction of gold from gold ORE. The rock is crushed and mixed with mercury to form a gold/mercury amalgam. It is then heated to burn off the mercury to leave the gold behind. This method causes major ecological problems because mercury is highly toxic and the waste poisons the rivers.

Answer to Algebra question on page 20:
The original equation was $3x+1=7$. The second illustration shows that if we take 1 from each side $3x=6$. If you divide each side by 3, $x=2$.

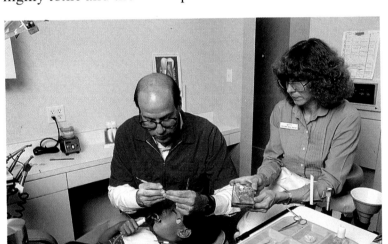

◄ Amalgams have been used for filling teeth cavities since the 19th century. Nowadays hard, plastic material the colour of teeth is more commonly used.

NH_3

▲ Ammonia is one of the most important compounds of the element nitrogen. It contains three atoms of hydrogen to each one of nitrogen.

Amino Acids *See* Protein

Ammonia

Ammonia is a colourless GAS with a sharp smell that irritates the eyes and nose. It is a chemical COMPOUND consisting of one ATOM of nitrogen and three atoms of hydrogen. Ammonia is lighter than air and burns in pure oxygen with a dull yellow flame. It does not burn in air. Ammonia becomes liquid at $-33.35°C$ and when it turns back into a gas again it takes in a large amount of HEAT from its surroundings. This makes liquid ammonia very useful as a cooling agent in REFRIGERATION equipment. Ammonia in solution is used for cleaning and removing

▲ Ammonia is often used in the manufacture of fertilizers. It contains nitrogen, which is important for plant growth.

23

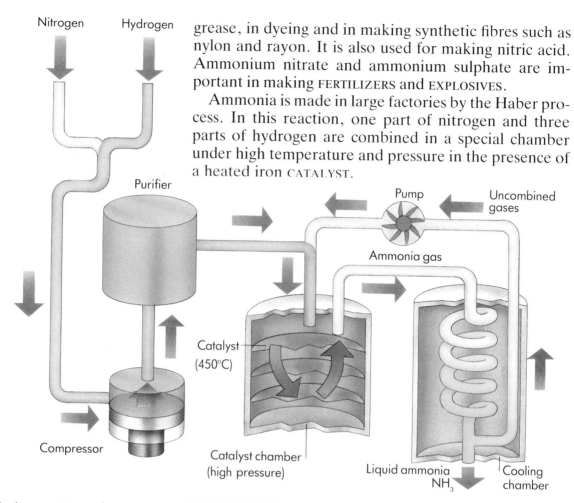

grease, in dyeing and in making synthetic fibres such as nylon and rayon. It is also used for making nitric acid. Ammonium nitrate and ammonium sulphate are important in making FERTILIZERS and EXPLOSIVES.

Ammonia is made in large factories by the Haber process. In this reaction, one part of nitrogen and three parts of hydrogen are combined in a special chamber under high temperature and pressure in the presence of a heated iron CATALYST.

▲ Ammonia is made commercially by the Haber process. A catalyst is used because it speeds up the reaction between nitrogen and hydrogen without itself being used up. Not all the nitrogen and hydrogen combine and any uncombined gases are reused.

Ampere

The ampere is the scientific unit for the strength of an electric current. It is usually shortened to amp. Using the 240-volt mains ELECTRICITY common in many countries, an ordinary electric bulb, for example, uses about one quarter of an amp, and an electric fire between 4 and 12 amps. Meters which are used to measure electric current are called *ammeters*.

See also FUSE; MAGNETISM.

André Ampère (1775–1836)
Ampère was a French physicist. He is famous for his work with electricity and magnetism. Ampère discovered that parallel electric currents attract each other if they move in the same direction, and repel each other if they move in opposite directions. He discovered that electricity produces magnetism and that when electricity is passed through a coiled wire it acts like a magnet. The unit used to measure the size of an electric current was named ampere, or amp, in his honour.

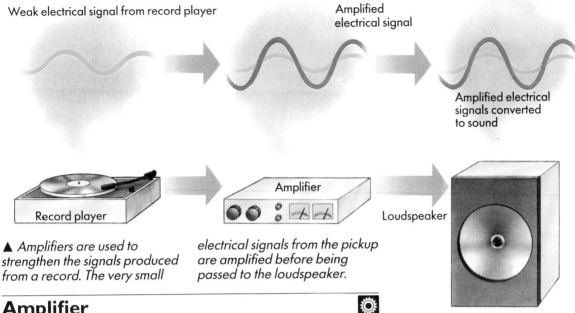

Weak electrical signal from record player

Amplified electrical signal

Amplified electrical signals converted to sound

Record player

Amplifier

Loudspeaker

▲ *Amplifiers are used to strengthen the signals produced from a record. The very small* *electrical signals from the pickup are amplified before being passed to the loudspeaker.*

Amplifier

An amplifier is a device for increasing the power of an electrical signal. They are found in electrical equipment such as radios, televisions and record players. A guitarist in a band will use an amplifier to increase the tiny electrical sound signals from the guitar's pickups and from the MICROPHONE so that they are powerful enough to drive sets of speakers that can fill a stadium with SOUND.

Deep SPACE PROBES such as *Voyager* and SATELLITES in orbit around the Earth send back signals that are so weak that the information cannot be understood until the signal strength has been amplified many times.
See also ELECTRICITY; HI-FI; LOUDSPEAKER.

Lee De Forest (1826–1906)
This American inventor pioneered wireless telegraphy and radio broadcasting. He invented a vacuum tube that amplified electrical symbols, which was to be significant in the development of radio and television communication.

Analogue

An analogue is an object or quantity that is similar to another object or quantity. The voltage passing through the TEMPERATURE sensor in an electric THERMOMETER rises and falls smoothly with the temperature change. The sensor current is an electrical analogue of the temperature and so it can be used to measure the temperature.

Biologists also use the word analogue to describe similarities between living creatures. The legs of a fly are 'analogous' to the legs of a cow, because both serve the same purpose. They both support the weight of the animal, but they have very different structures.
See also DIGITAL.

▲ *An analogue device.*

Different methods are used to find out what substances are made of.
Electronanalysis is used to find out how a substance reacts to an electric current.
Chromatography is a technique that may be used to separate a substance into its component parts before it is analysed.
Spectrometry can be used to find out what a substance is by examining the spectrum of light or other electromagnetic radiation it gives off.

Analysis, chemical

Chemical analysis is the process used to find out the exact make-up of a substance. The substance has to be examined in very great detail using a number of different methods. There are two main types of analysis: qualitative and quantitative. *Qualitative analysis* is used to discover which ELEMENTS or groups of elements make up the substance under examination. *Quantitative analysis* is the process of measuring the amounts, or proportions of the elements in the substance. In qualitative analysis, a sample of the substance may be heated to see what is given off, it may be held in a flame (a flame test), or it may be dissolved in water and treated with various agents to find out how it reacts. In quantitative analysis, once the ingredients of a substance are known, they must be measured using extremely accurate measuring devices. Analysis is of great importance in diagnosing DISEASE, preparing medicines and testing for POLLUTION or acidity levels in soil or air.

Flame Test
Flame tests are used to identify chemical elements by seeing which colour they give off when held in the flame of a Bunsen burner. A compound of an element is burned on the end of a piece of platinum wire or asbestos. The flame burns a distinctive colour and so the element can be identified.

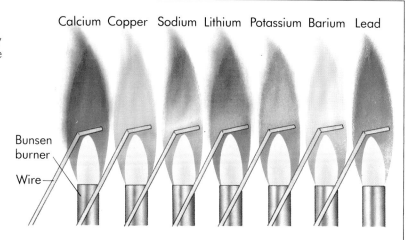

Calcium Copper Sodium Lithium Potassium Barium Lead

Bunsen burner

Wire

Adults have 206 bones in their bodies (children have more but some fuse together as they grow). These bones make up the skeleton, which has three main functions. It protects important organs, such as the heart, lungs and the brain. It allows the person to stand upright, and provides attachment points for the muscles.

Anatomy

Anatomy is the study of the structure of living things. By knowing how organisms are constructed, we are able to discover and understand how they work. Doctors study the structure of the human body including the SKELETON, MUSCLES, blood vessels and NERVES as well as all the internal organs so they know how the body functions in health and illness. Zoologists and vets study the anatomy of other animals. Botanists study plant anatomy, the structure of plants including the FLOWERS, STEMS,

LEAVES and ROOTS as well as all the complex internal systems.
See also BOTANY; MEDICINE; PHYSIOLOGY; ZOOLOGY.

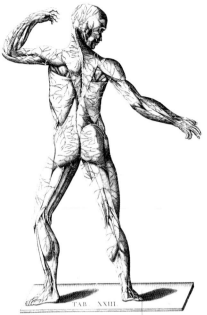

▲ *This 16th-century anatomical drawing suggests positions for a human's nerves and muscles.*

◄ *Plant anatomy has been studied for centuries. This drawing of the nutmeg dates from 1795.*

Anemia (Anaemia) *See* Blood

Anemometer

An anemometer is an instrument which is used in METEOROLOGY to measure the speed of the WIND. It is usually mounted on a mast and positioned so that the wind blows freely around it. The most common type has three or four cone-shaped cups at the end of arms that rotate as the wind blows. The faster the wind blows, the faster the cups rotate. Wind speed can be measured by the number of REVOLUTIONS per minute.

Anode *See* Electrolysis

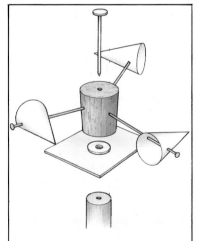

SEE FOR YOURSELF
To make an anemometer make 3 cardboard cones. Push a pin through each one into a cork. Next insert a long nail through the cork, a metal washer and a piece of card and fix to the top of a wooden pole. The faster the wind blows, the faster the cones will rotate.

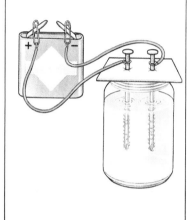

Anodizing

Anodizing is a process in which a protective coating of an oxide, is placed on a metal. This is done by putting the metal, usually ALUMINIUM, into a special liquid and passing an electric current through the liquid. By anodizing metal, it is possible to produce a surface on it that cannot be scratched or rubbed off.

There are other benefits of anodizing metal. It makes the metal resistant to CORROSION. Anodized metal is used in aircraft, trains and ships. One common use for anodizing is in making aluminium window frames. Aluminium is light and strong, but it turns white and dull when exposed to the damp. Anodizing coats it with a very hard layer of oxide less than a hundredth of a millimetre thick, so that the surface still stays bright.
See also ELECTROLYSIS.

Antenna

An antenna is a long thin growth on the head of an insect, snail or shellfish, used to sense the world around the animal. Antennae (the plural of antenna) usually occur in pairs. The end of each antenna carries organs for sensing touch, taste or smell.

In a RADIO or TELEVISION system, an antenna (or aerial) transmits or receives radio waves. At the transmitter it turns electrical signals into radio waves. At the receiver it turns radio waves back into electrical signals. The antenna may be made from a length of wire, a metal rod or a branched structure of metal struts. Its shape depends on the signal it is designed to receive. A dish-shaped antenna is used to receive very weak signals. The

▲ *This black fly has been greatly magnified using an electron microscope. It uses its antennae to detect danger.*

▶ *Antennae transmit and receive different kinds of radio waves.*

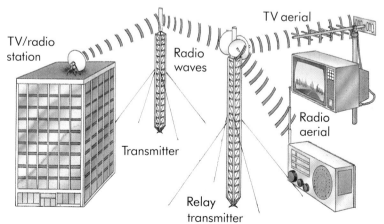

dish acts like a mirror and reflects radio signals inward towards a small antenna at the centre of the dish, called the FOCUS. From there the signals are amplified and passed to a receiver. The biggest dish antenna (304.8 m across), used by astronomers to receive radio signals from distant stars, was built in a natural valley near Arecibo in Puerto Rico in 1963.

Antibiotics

Antibiotics can be used to treat many diseases in both animals and humans. These drugs attack MICROORGAN-ISMS such as bacteria, which are the cause of infections such as tonsillitis and boils. Antibiotics work very well against bacteria, but have almost no effect at all against VIRUSES which are the other common cause of infection.

Antibiotics work by damaging the bacteria as they reproduce and do not usually damage human cells.

Alexander Fleming (1881–1955)
Fleming was a British bacteriologist. In 1928 he noticed that a spot of green mould stopped the growth of some bacteria he was cultivating. The antibiotic drug penicillin was developed from the mould. Fleming won the 1945 Nobel Prize for medicine, which he shared with Howard Florey and Ernst Chain, the scientists who developed the use of the drug.

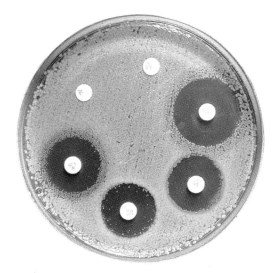

◄ This dish contains bacteria. The circles contain different antibiotics. Four antibiotics have killed the bacteria around them, but the other two have not.

Bacteria have a rigid cell wall, which gives them a firm shape and protects them from the body's defences. They reproduce by dividing and re-forming their cell walls as two new cells. The antibiotics hinder this process. This may either kill the bacteria or weaken them so that the body's IMMUNE SYSTEM can easily destroy them.

The first antibiotics were discovered by accident and extracted from tiny fungi called moulds. Penicillin, from the fungus *Penicillium*, was the first of these. Many different antibiotics are now available to treat a wide variety of microorganisms.

See also MEDICINE; REPRODUCTION.

In 1941, a British policeman became the first person to be treated with the antibiotic penicillin. The patient was suffering from bacterial blood poisoning and after a dose of penicillin, he started to make a recovery. Despite his initial recovery, he died because there was not enough penicillin available to kill all the infectious bacteria.

1 *Bacteria invade the blood and produce toxins. They both infect the blood.*

2 *In defence, white blood cells produce antibodies, which recognize the antigens.*

3 *The antibodies attack the antigens and capture them by locking onto them.*

4 *White blood cells engulf the bacteria and toxins, break them up and digest them.*

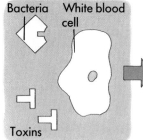
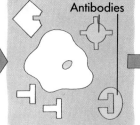
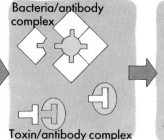
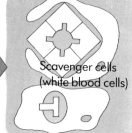

▲ *The steps taken by white blood cells to defend the body against infection.*

SEE FOR YOURSELF
Float an ice cube in a bowl of water. Place a matchstick on top of the ice cube and sprinkle some salt around it. Salt causes the ice on each side of the matchstick to melt. This is because salt water freezes at a lower temperature than ordinary water. No salt falls under the matchstick and so the stick stands out on a ridge of ice. In the same way, salt is sometimes used on roads as an antifreeze protection to stop ice forming.

Antibodies and Antigens

An antibody is produced by the body to fight against invading organisms or substances which could be harmful. Antibodies are PROTEINS, which are produced in great numbers in the body by some white blood cells. An antibody is able to recognise an antigen (the substance it is to attack). The antigen may be part of the cell wall of a bacterium, part of a VIRUS, or it could be a chemical substance which has entered the system.

An antibody MOLECULE is shaped so that it can attach itself firmly to the antigen rather like a key entering a lock. The antigen becomes covered with a mass of antibodies, which makes it harmless. It is then either broken down or consumed by scavenging white blood cells.

Once the body has learned how to deal with a particular type of invading organism by producing antibodies to attack it, it can produce them again very quickly if the same organism enters the body. In this way, we become immune to an INFECTION, which normally prevents us from catching the same infection again.

See also ALLERGY; BLOOD; IMMUNE SYSTEM; VACCINATION.

Antifreeze

Antifreeze is a liquid that is added to water to lower its FREEZING POINT. Many antifreezes also raise the BOILING POINTS of liquids too. The most common liquid used as an antifreeze is the ALCOHOL, ethanediol (ethylene glycol). Antifreeze is used in de-icing compounds and refrigerants. It is most commonly used in the water cooling systems of motor vehicles.

An engine runs at very high temperatures and needs

to be cooled, usually by water which is circulated through the system. It is necessary to add antifreeze to the water to prevent the water FREEZING in cold temperatures. When water freezes it expands in volume, and if this happens in a pipe or the engine block of a vehicle, it can cause the metal to split or crack, ruining the engine. *See also* MIXTURES.

Antihistamines *See* Allergy

Antimatter

Antimatter is MATTER made up of SUBATOMIC PARTICLES that are exactly the same as the particles commonly found, except that they have the opposite charge. They are called antiparticles. An ELECTRON, for example, is an ordinary particle which has a negative charge. Its antiparticle, a kind of 'anti'-electron called a POSITRON, is the same as the electron in every way except that it carries a positive charge. If you think of an ordinary ATOM, it is made up of PROTONS, NEUTRONS and electrons. An antiatom would be made up of anti-protons, anti-neutrons and positrons. Antimatter was first described in 1930 before anyone had discovered or produced it. Antiparticles can be produced using a PARTICLE ACCELERATOR.

Antiseptics

Antiseptics are substances which kill or prevent the growth of germs (DISEASE-producing organisms) on skin and mucous-membranes. They have to be mild enough not to irritate the SKIN or membranes. There are

Disinfectant A liquid that destroys or inhibits the activity of germs on non-living things.
Infection An illness caused by a disease-carrying organism.
Septic A condition caused when bacteria rot or decay living matter.
Septicaemia A disease caused by contamination of the bloodstream by infectious bacteria.

▲ This carbolic acid spray was the first successful antiseptic used in hospitals. Previously, antiseptics such as wine, tar, turpentine and mercury had been used to kill germs, but they often harmed the patients.

Joseph Lister (1827–1912)
Lister was a British surgeon who radically changed surgical practice with the introduction of antiseptics. They reduced the risk of bacterial infection during surgery. Lister's antiseptic solution of carbolic acid was used to clean wounds and surgical cuts and to scrub surgeons' hands. Lister believed that infection was caused by airborne dust particles, so he also sprayed the air with carbolic acid. The equipment was heated to a high temperature to make it bacteria free. His discoveries met with initial resistance but had become widely accepted by the 1880s when he introduced antiseptic catgut ligatures. Ligatures are the strong threads used to sew surgical wounds together. He also devised new operations and invented several surgical instruments.

It is believed that divers first used snorkels, made of hollow reeds, in about AD 100. Independent breathing devices for diving, which were the forerunners of the aqualung, were tested during the late 1800s and 1900s.

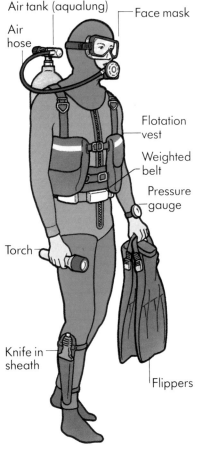

Air tank (aqualung)

Air hose

Face mask

Flotation vest

Weighted belt

Pressure gauge

Torch

Knife in sheath

Flippers

▲ *Aqualungs are essential equipment for divers. The one shown here is an open circuit system, where the air is exhaled into the water instead of being re-used.*

▶ *The invention of scuba equipment has provided the diver with greater mobility and range.*

many different chemicals that are used as antiseptics, including some ALCOHOLS. The many different kinds of antiseptic products available include mouthwashes, soaps, creams and ointments.

The most common use for antiseptics is in the first-aid treatment of wounds. If you graze yourself, you may use an antiseptic, diluted with water, to clean away dirt from the area of the wound and kill any germs on the surface of the skin. Surgeons use antiseptics to scrub their hands and to prepare the patient's skin before an operation so bacteria will not cause an INFECTION.

Antiseptics were introduced into surgery in the late 1860s by Joseph Lister and the number of deaths resulting from infection fell dramatically. In modern operating theatres, surgical instruments are sterilized by heat under pressure in an autoclave.

See also MEDICINE; STERILIZATION.

Aqualung

An aqualung is a metal tank, full of compressed AIR, that can be easily strapped to the back of a diver. This enables him or her to breathe underwater for up to an hour at a time. The air in the tank passes through a pipe to the mouthpiece. A demand valve releases the air only when the diver breathes in so that he or she can breathe normally. The first aqualung was successfully tested in 1943 by Jacques Cousteau. It is often called scuba equipment, (self-contained underwater breathing apparatus).

Even with an aqualung it is rare that a diver goes below about 30 m because of problems caused by the enormous PRESSURE of the water on the diver's body. Water pressure is greater than ATMOSPHERIC pressure and increases with depth. If a diver comes to the surface too quickly after a deep dive the nitrogen which has been compressed, bubbles in the bloodstream causing an agonizing and very dangerous condition called the 'bends'. This is avoided by rising very slowly, with occasional stops, to allow the body to release the nitrogen slowly.

Archimedes

Archimedes (c.287–212 BC) was a Greek mathematician and inventor who lived in Syracuse, Sicily. His work led him to make some important basic scientific discoveries.

His most famous invention was the Archimedean screw, a rotating device for raising water or grain. In places where pumps are not available, these are still used

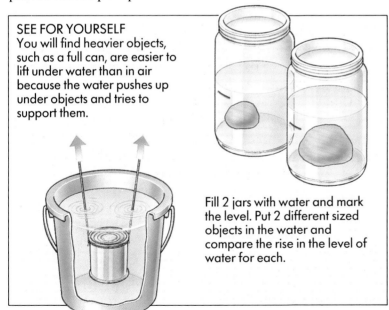

SEE FOR YOURSELF
You will find heavier objects, such as a full can, are easier to lift under water than in air because the water pushes up under objects and tries to support them.

Fill 2 jars with water and mark the level. Put 2 different sized objects in the water and compare the rise in the level of water for each.

▲ Archimedes, a Greek mathematician and inventor tested his ideas by experimentation.

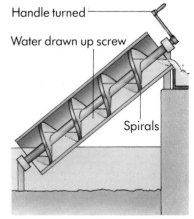

▼ The Archimedean screw has been in use for centuries. It is used to lift water from a low to a high level. One end of the screw is placed in the water. As the handle is turned, the screw inside the cylinder revolves and the water is carried upwards. The casing must fit tightly to prevent leakage.

Handle turned

Water drawn up screw

Spirals

to lift water for irrigation. He also worked out the laws of LEVERS and PULLEYS. One well-known story about Archimedes says that one day he got into a bath and it overflowed. He jumped out and ran through the town shouting 'Eureka!' (Greek for 'I have found it!'). He had suddenly realized how to measure the volume of gold in the King's crown. If he put it into a vessel full to the brim with water, the water that overflowed would be the same volume as the crown. *See also* FLOTATION.

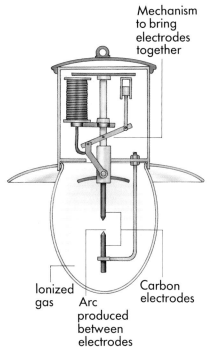

Mechanism to bring electrodes together

Ionized gas

Arc produced between electrodes

Carbon electrodes

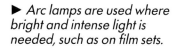

▲ The arc lamp was one of the earliest electric lights.

► Arc lamps are used where bright and intense light is needed, such as on film sets.

▲ Aristarchus, a Greek astronomer who lived on Samos in around 300 BC.

Arc lamp

An arc lamp produces a very bright light when an electric current jumps, or arcs, across the space between two CARBON rods called electrodes. The tips of the carbon rods become white hot and begin to burn away. A mechanism keeps the burning tips of the rods the right distance apart. The first lamp of this kind was invented by Thomas Wright in 1845, but early arc lamps needed a great deal of electrical power. In 1856 an Englishman, Frederick Homes, tried using an electricity GENERATOR to power arc lamps for use in lighthouses. His system was later used at Souter Point in Northumberland, England.

Carbon-arc lamps have now been superseded by other forms of lighting such as sodium-arc and mercury-arc lamps for powerful outdoor lighting.

See also ELECTRIC ARC; ELECTRICITY.

Aristarchus

Aristarchus was a Greek astronomer who was born about 300 BC. He is believed to be the first person who thought that the EARTH revolved around the SUN. In those days the Earth was considered fixed at the centre of the UNIVERSE. Almost two thousand years later, scientists realized he was right.

Before TELESCOPES had been invented, Aristarchus made important observations with the naked eye. For example, by observations he proved that the Sun must be much further away than the Moon. He also tried to measure the length of the year to an accuracy of one minute.

His opinion that the Earth moves around the Sun

made him unpopular, and he risked being arrested for teaching false beliefs. But he is remembered as one of the very first 'scientists' (people who try to show that an idea must be supported by observed evidence).
See also COPERNICUS; GALILEO; SOLAR SYSTEM.

Aristotle

Aristotle (384–322 BC) was a Greek philosopher and scientist. He was a pupil of the famous Greek philosopher Plato. Aristotle was keen on observing and cataloguing what he saw in nature. Most Greeks of the time believed that the basic facts about the world could be discovered by thinking about them rather than by observation and EXPERIMENTATION as the modern scientist does. He also pondered mathematical and astronomical problems, ethics (right and wrong), politics and law.

Aristotle's reputation grew after his death. This probably slowed down scientific progress. For example, believing him to be right in suggesting that all heavenly bodies move in circles, astronomers tried in vain for 17 centuries, to explain the PLANETS' movements.

▲ *Aristotle, the Greek thinker, is also regarded as the first great biologist. He thought everything was made up of four main elements: earth, fire, air and water and their properties, dry, hot, cold and wet.*

▼ *Aristotle divided the animal world into different categories, depending on how the animals' offspring were produced.*

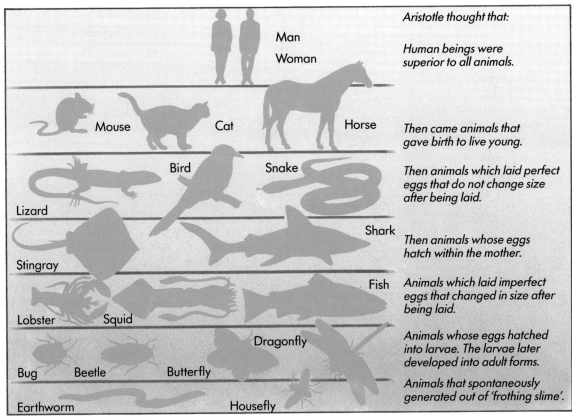

Man
Woman

Aristotle thought that:

Human beings were superior to all animals.

Mouse   Cat   Horse

Then came animals that gave birth to live young.

Bird   Snake

Then animals which laid perfect eggs that do not change size after being laid.

Lizard

Shark

Then animals whose eggs hatch within the mother.

Stingray

Fish

Animals which laid imperfect eggs that changed in size after being laid.

Lobster   Squid

Dragonfly

Animals whose eggs hatched into larvae. The larvae later developed into adult forms.

Bug   Beetle   Butterfly

Earthworm   Housefly

Animals that spontaneously generated out of 'frothing slime'.

SEE FOR YOURSELF
How many grains of rice will there be on the 11th square of a chessboard if I place one on the first, two on the second, four on the third, eight on the fourth and so on? Answer on page 38.

Arithmetic is used to solve problems using numbers. It comes from a Greek word *arithmetike, arithmos*, meaning number and *techne*, meaning art or skill. Different number systems have been developed by different civilizations. The most common system is the one in which objects are counted in groups of 10. These are known as decimal systems, or base 10 arithmetic.

▶ *Arithmetic has been used since ancient times to solve mathematical problems. This Egyptian papyrus dates from 1650 BC. It was copied from an even older papyrus written between 1849 and 1801 BC. It is full of problems for students, exactly like those we do in school today.*

▲ *This picture shows a crystal cluster of arsenic trisulphide. It was once thought to contain gold because of its colour.*

Arithmetic

Arithmetic is a branch of MATHEMATICS that helps us to use NUMBERS to solve problems which may be practical ones, such as how large the area of a field is, or more complex. Arithmetic lets us use numbers in four ways. We can add them together, take one away from another one, multiply them together, or divide one by another. These separate actions are known as addition, subtraction, multiplication and division.

Arithmetic involves working with parts of numbers, such as fractions, DECIMALS and percentages, and measures to find out lengths, areas and volumes. The Babylonians were among the first to use arithmetic about 4000 years ago. They counted in sixties. The Hindus invented the system that we now use, called Arabic numerals because the Arabs brought them to Europe.

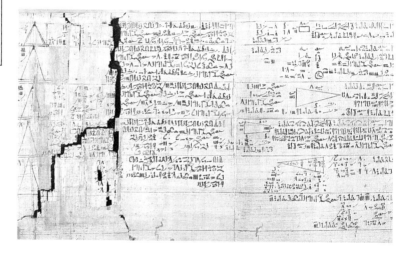

Arsenic

Arsenic is a semi-metallic chemical ELEMENT with three solid forms: grey arsenic, yellow arsenic and black arsenic. Grey arsenic is the most stable form. It is shiny in appearance, quite a good conductor of HEAT and ELECTRICITY, but it breaks easily. At 613°C grey arsenic sublimes (the solid form turns into a vapour without becoming a liquid first). Arsenic is usually extracted from the rocks in which it is found by roasting the rocks in air. The arsenic combines with the oxygen in the air, and this oxygen can later be removed. Arsenic is very poisonous and if taken in small doses over a long period it can cause cancer. Since ancient times arsenic has been used in making poisons, medicines and artists' colours. Today, it is used mainly in insecticides, rat poisons and weed killers, in LASERS, TRANSISTORS and other electrical devices, and for toughening alloys.

Artery *See* Circulation

Artesian well

An artesian well is a borehole in a layer of porous rock such as sandstone, limestone or CHALK. Artesian wells are found throughout most of the world because large amounts of WATER soak into the Earth's surface.

Water collects in areas of high rainfall and flows down into the porous rock layer. If it is sealed above and below by layers of clay or impermeable rocks (that do not let water through), the water then accumulates in the porous layer (the water table). The water lower down in the sealed rock layer (an aquifer) is under PRESSURE from the water above. When a hole is drilled the pressure will force water to the surface. Sometimes water is drawn from the aquifer faster than it is replaced. In this case, the pressure drops and water cannot be raised to the surface without pumps. Nowadays, pumps are often used.

Permeable A material such as sandstone that allows air, water or other fluids to pass through it.
Impermeable A material that does not allow water or other fluids to pass through.
Water table The highest level in the porous layer of ground that is filled (saturated) with water.
Aquifer A layer of porous material such as rock, sand or gravel filled with ground water.

▼ *Pumps are used to draw water up from the artesian well when the water table is low. The name 'Artesian' comes from a region in France called Artois. The oldest artesian well in Europe is believed to have been dug there in 1126. Below is an artesian well showing how water collects between layers of rock.*

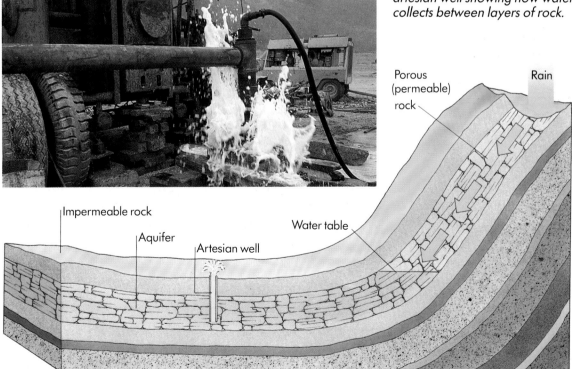

Porous (permeable) rock

Rain

Impermeable rock

Aquifer

Artesian well

Water table

Scientists have produced machines that can easily recognize and read printed words (optical character recognition). The pattern of each character is scanned with a laser and compared with patterns that have already been programmed into the machine. Programming the machine to recognize new patterns is a long and painstaking process.

Answer to Arithmetic question on page 36:
On the 11th square there will be 1024 grains of rice, too many to fit on a chess board square. By the 21st square there will be over a million.

▶ *When playing noughts and crosses a computer assesses all possible moves at each stage. It assigns each move a value; +1 for a win, 0 for a draw and –1 for a loss. Each move is then tried out and the one that gives the best score is taken. The computer's moves (X) are mapped out on the right.*

▼ *Here a computer is being used to test an autopilot, a device which can fly an aircraft.*

Arthritis *See Joints*

Artificial intelligence

Artificial intelligence is the performance by COMPUTERS of tasks that seem to require INTELLIGENCE. It is as if the computer can think for itself, but we know that any computer can only follow a series of operations laid down in programs written by computer programmers. Research

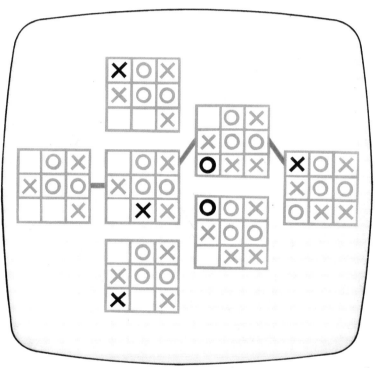

in this area concentrates on getting computers to solve problems. This has led to the development of computers that can, for example, calculate where best to drill for oil, how to diagnose medical conditions and even how to fly aircraft. In order to make these decisions, the computer has to be given vast amounts of information.

Experiments are under way to link cameras with computers so that they can identify shapes. Sound links enable computers to recognize human speech so that instructions can be spoken to a computer instead of entering them through a keyboard. The whole area of 'expert systems', where computers help us to make important decisions by analysing masses of information quickly and accurately, already plays an important part in industrial development.

See also COMPUTER LANGUAGES; COMPUTER MEMORY.

Asbestos

Asbestos is a soft and threadlike MINERAL noted for its resistance to BURNING. It is extracted from certain rocks. It was once used for a variety of purposes, including fire-proof clothes and as insulating material. Now its use is severely limited because the fibres that it produces and releases into the air can damage the LUNGS if they are breathed in for a long time. This fatal disease is called asbestosis.

See also INSULATION, THERMAL.

Asteroid

An asteroid is a tiny PLANET that revolves around the SUN. Most of them can be found in the wide gap between the orbits of MARS and JUPITER. The largest asteroid, Ceres, is 1000 km across, but most are much smaller.

Some asteroids have unusual orbits. Chiron is further from the Sun than SATURN. Others come inside the Earth's orbit, and may pass near us. The closest recorded encounter happened on 22 March 1989, when a tiny asteroid, now called 1989 FC, passed at less than twice the distance to the Moon.

Most asteroids are thought to have formed when specks of dust orbiting the Sun in a vast cloud formed small clumps, which collected together and grew in size.

There are so many asteroids that naming them is difficult. Most commemorate people, but No. 3568 has been named after the computer character code ASCII!

▲ All asteroids whose orbits cross the Earth's orbit are called apollo asteroids. The name comes from the first asteroid discovered to have this orbit. Asteroids are not round in shape but have a very irregular surface.

▼ Most known asteroids orbit the Sun in a belt between Mars and Jupiter. Asteroids are also called minor planets.

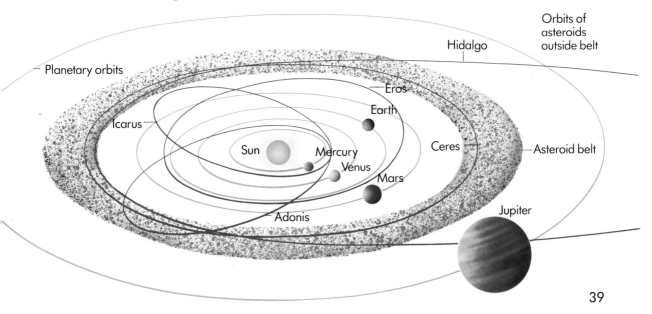

Orbits of asteroids outside belt

Hidalgo

Planetary orbits

Eros

Earth

Icarus

Sun   Mercury   Ceres   Asteroid belt

Venus

Mars

Adonis

Jupiter

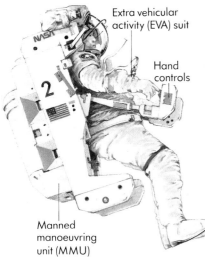

Extra vehicular activity (EVA) suit

Hand controls

Manned manoeuvring unit (MMU)

▲ *Bruce McCandless was the first astronaut ever to use an MMU. For work outside the spacecraft, an astronaut wears an EVA suit.*

Astronaut

An astronaut is someone who is trained to travel in space. More than 200 people have been launched into space since the Soviet pilot Yuri Gagarin made the first orbit of Earth on 12 April 1961 and began the age of SPACE EXPLORATION.

Astronauts must be extremely fit to survive the tremendous force of lift-off, which makes the body feel as if it is being squashed. An astronaut is trained to operate spacecraft controls and carry out complicated tasks in difficult conditions. These tasks could include performing experiments for scientists on the ground, launching new SATELLITES, or even rescuing damaged ones for repair.

In space, everything in the cabin is weightless. This affects the human body, which is used to fighting GRAVITY. Muscles are not used as much, and they will begin to waste away without regular exercise. Keeping astronauts healthy (SPACE MEDICINE) is important. Eating and drinking present problems since water breaks up into floating droplets, and a haze of crumbs and debris would form. Therefore an astronaut has to squeeze food into his or her mouth from sachets and suck liquid through a straw.

Underneath the EVA suit

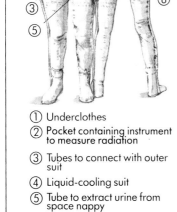

① Underclothes
② Pocket containing instrument to measure radiation
③ Tubes to connect with outer suit
④ Liquid-cooling suit
⑤ Tube to extract urine from space nappy
⑥ Tubes containing water

Space food

Plastic tube

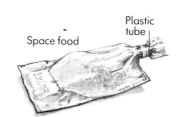

▲ *An astronaut's food must be easy to eat and store, as well as nutritious. Food is freeze-dried and the astronaut only needs to add water to make it ready to eat.*

▶ *A view of Earth that astronauts see from space.*

Some Famous Astronauts
12 April 1961 Yuri Gagarin first orbits the Earth.
16 June 1963 Valentina Tereshkova first woman in space.
21 July 1969 Neil Armstrong and Edwin Aldrin make the first manned Moon landing.
15 July 1975 Vance Brand, Donald Slayton, Thomas Stafford, Alexei Leonov and Valery Kubasov in first international space mission.
12 April 1981 John Young and Robert Crippen make first Space Shuttle flight.

ASTRONOMY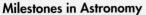

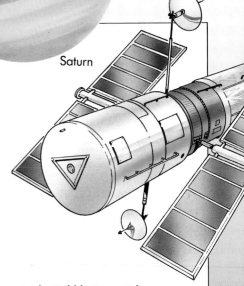

Saturn

The Earth is a tiny speck in space. If you imagine it shrunk down to a diameter of one millimetre, the Sun's nearest neighbouring star would be 3000 km away. The remotest visible galaxies are so distant that the light they send out takes about 10,000 million years to reach us, even though light can travel seven times round the Earth in one second.

Astronomers survey this huge volume of space, where there are many different things to study. Our nearest star, the Sun, sends out light and heat to make life on Earth possible. It also shines on the other eight major planets and numerous other tiny bodies (over 50 satellites, thousands of asteroids or 'minor planets', and possibly a million comets) in the Solar System.

In our galaxy, there are 100,000 million stars. Some, the 'dwarfs', are much dimmer than the Sun, while the 'giants' are far brighter. Many stars are in clusters containing from 50 to 100,000 members, and there are also vast clouds of gas and dust, known as 'nebulae', in which new stars are being born. Millions of other galaxies, some smaller and some larger than our own, can be detected. They are moving apart like particles in an explosion suggesting that the Universe started with a 'big bang'.

▲ The Hubble Space Telescope can send us pictures of distant objects because it is above the Earth's atmosphere.

▲ A radio telescope collects and records radio waves that come from objects in space.

Milestones in Astronomy
270 BC Aristarchus teaches that the Earth orbits the Sun.
1608 Lippershey invents the telescope.
1600s Kepler proposes that the planets' orbits are ellipses.
1687 Newton publishes theory of gravity.
1920 Distant galaxies are discovered to be flying away at great speeds.
1929 Hubble demonstrates that the Universe is expanding.
1963 Background radiation, thought to be from the Big Bang, is discovered.
1992 Ripples in background radiation confirm Big Bang theory.

SEE FOR YOURSELF
By using a pair of binoculars you can make your own astronomical observations at night. NEVER look at the Sun. Record what you see at the same time every evening. Keep the electric light off so that your eyes grow accustomed to the dim light. Use a bicycle lamp covered with red see-through paper so you can see to write.

◄ People have been studying the stars for centuries. These Turkish astronomers are observing the planets and stars during the Middle Ages.

See also ASTEROID; BIG BANG THEORY; BIG CRUNCH; BLACK HOLE; COMETS; GALAXY; NEBULA; PLANETS; SOLAR SYSTEM; STARS; UNIVERSE.

▶ *The atmosphere is held close to the Earth by gravity. It is divided into various layers according to differences in temperature. The troposphere, in which we live, contains more than 75 percent of the atmosphere. Nearly all the clouds, rain and snow occur in this layer. The stratosphere extends up to 48 km above the Earth. Clouds are rare and aircraft usually fly in this layer above the weather disturbances in the troposphere. The ozone layer is between the stratosphere and the mesosphere. The mesosphere extends to 80 km above the Earth. Above this lies the thermosphere where the air is very thin. Over 99.99 percent of the atmosphere lies below it. The lower part of the thermosphere, the ionosphere, reflects radio waves back to Earth so signals can be sent round the world. The exosphere begins about 480 km above the Earth and fades away into space.*

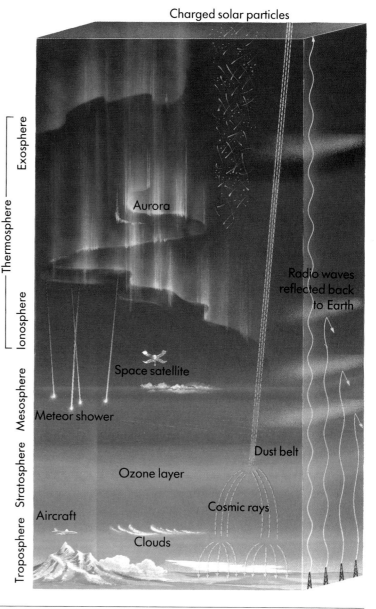

Charged solar particles

Aurora

Radio waves reflected back to Earth

Space satellite

Meteor shower

Dust belt

Ozone layer

Cosmic rays

Aircraft

Clouds

Atmosphere — Exosphere / Thermosphere / Ionosphere / Mesosphere / Stratosphere / Troposphere

---

The mixture of gases in the atmosphere has taken over 4.5 billion years to evolve. About 99 percent of the atmosphere is made up of nitrogen and oxygen. The gases in the remaining one percent are argon, carbon dioxide and tiny amounts of hydrogen, ozone, methane, carbon monoxide, helium, neon, krypton and xenon. The amount of water vapour depends on temperature and humidity.

Atmosphere

The atmosphere is a band of gas known as AIR, surrounding the Earth. It extends from the Earth's surface into outer space. It is made up of about 78 percent nitrogen, 21 percent oxygen and 1 percent other gases.

The atmosphere also exerts PRESSURE. Atmospheric pressure is produced by the weight of the air at the top of the band as it presses down on the air below. It presses onto the surface of the Earth with a force about one kilogram on each square centimetre. We do not notice this tremendous pressure though it is present all the time.

The atmosphere becomes thinner and harder to

breathe at high altitudes. This is because less air is pressing down from above. Traces of atmosphere can be detected for thousands of kilometres into space, but even at the height of Mexico City (2200 m) some athletes in the 1968 Olympics suffered from breathlessness.

As well as becoming thinner, the higher atmosphere is cold. At the height of Everest (8848 m) the air temperature is −50°C. For both these reasons aircraft need to be airtight and supplied with their own oxygen as well as being insulated against the cold.

The atmosphere protects us by blocking out dangerous RADIATION from the SUN and space. For example, a layer of oxygen called the OZONE LAYER cuts out invisible light (ULTRAVIOLET) that could cause fatal sunburn. *See also* BAROMETER; BOILING POINT.

Scientists have worked out that if the carbon dioxide content in the Earth's atmosphere was doubled to 0.06 percent, the over-all temperature of the Earth would rise. This would cause the ice caps to melt and the low coastal areas to flood.

Atom

An atom is a minute unit of MATTER. Atoms are so tiny that about a million of them would fit onto the full stop at the end of this sentence. Everything around us is made up of atoms. Atoms contain even tinier particles called PROTONS, NEUTRONS and ELECTRONS. These have different arrangements in different chemical ELEMENTS. There are more than 100 chemical elements existing in the UNIVERSE, each of which is made up of only one kind of atom. Hydrogen and oxygen are two examples. *See* pages 44-45.

Atom bomb See Hydrogen bomb

Atomic energy See Nuclear energy

Atomic number

The atomic number of a chemical ELEMENT gives us the number of positive charges or PROTONS there are in the atomic nucleus (or how many ELECTRONS there are spinning round it). The number is the same for both, so the ATOM has no charge. Carbon, for example has six protons and six electrons, therefore its atomic number is six.

The atoms of the 92 naturally-occurring elements can be placed in order by arranging them according to their atomic numbers. The atomic number determines an element's position in the PERIODIC TABLE. Elements with atomic numbers greater than 92 can be created artificially: Lawrencium has an atomic number of 103.

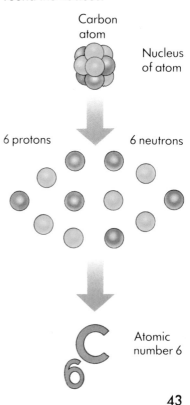

▼ Every element has its own atomic number. The atomic number is the same as the number of protons. The nucleus of a carbon atom has six protons and six neutrons, and so has an atomic number of six. It also has six electrons spinning round the nucleus.

Carbon atom

Nucleus of atom

6 protons　　6 neutrons

Atomic number 6

ATOM

More than 2000 years ago the Greeks argued about the make-up of matter. One group of philosophers, known as the atomists, believed that if you kept cutting something into smaller and smaller pieces, you would eventually get a tiny piece you could not cut. (The Greek word *atom* means 'uncut'.) The theory of the atom did not catch on until John Dalton developed his atomic theory. The discovery of the electron in 1897 proved that atoms are cuttable.

Atoms are made up of a system of tiny particles. Every atom has a nucleus, which contains protons and, except hydrogen, neutrons, with electrons spinning round it. A proton has a positive electrical charge, an electron has a negative charge, and a neutron has no charge at all. Each atom making up the same element has the same number of protons and electrons, so it is neither positive nor negative. An atom is made up of a large amount of empty space, but electrons travel at such a high speed that it makes an atom appear to behave like a solid (in the same way as a propeller blade turning at very high speed both looks solid and repels objects thrown against it). Individual atoms of the same or different elements can join together by sharing electrons to form molecules and also compounds.

▼ *If an atom were the size of your little finger nail, then your hand would be large enough to hold the Earth.*

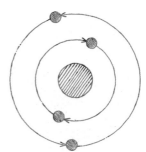

Bohr's model of the atom

Niels Bohr (1885–1962)
Bohr was a Danish physicist who contributed greatly to the development of modern nuclear physics. For his work on the structure of the atom he won the 1922 Nobel Prize for Physics. In 1943 he worked as an advisor to scientists developing the nuclear bomb.

◄ *Atoms are so small that they need to be magnified many times in order to be seen. The first pictures of individual atoms were taken in 1970 with an electron microscope, like the one pictured here.*

A tiny speck of dust, which is only just visible to the human eye, contains about 1000 million million (or a million billion) atoms.

Milestones in the study of the atom
400s BC Democritus gives the name atom to the basic particle.
1750 Boscovich believes atoms are made up of even smaller parts.
1803 Dalton proposes that each element has its own particular type of atom.
1911 Rutherford proposes that most of the mass of an atom is concentrated in a small nucleus consisting of protons, which is surrounded by electrons travelling at great speed.
1932 Chadwick discovers that the nucleus contains neutrons.
1938 Nuclear fission is discovered.
1971 Quarks identified. Shown to be smaller than protons and neutrons.
1988 Position (anti-electron) microscope in use.

Neon atom

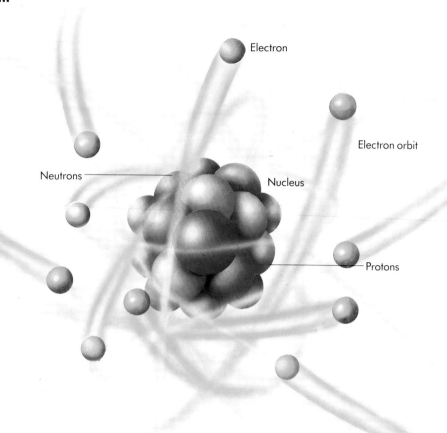

Electron

Electron orbit

Neutrons

Nucleus

Protons

▲ *Electrons constantly change their positions as they whizz round a nucleus of protons and neutrons, making billions of trips in one millionth of a second.*

▼ *An atom's nucleus contains energy that can be released to produce nuclear energy. The blue glow in the core of a nuclear reactor is produced by the atoms.*

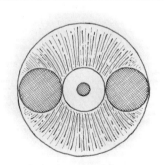

Dalton's model of the atom

John Dalton (1766–1844)
Dalton was an English chemist. He is best known for his atomic theory to explain the structure of matter. It became one of the foundations of modern chemistry. He was first to calculate the weights of the atoms of several elements. He worked out a table of atomic weights of elements but it was later found to be inaccurate.

See also ANTIMATTER; COMPOUNDS; ELEMENT; ELECTRON; ION; MOLECULE; NEUTRON; PROTON; SUBATOMIC PARTICLES.

Jons Berzelius (1779–1848)
Berzelius was a Swedish chemist. He classified different substances by calculating their atomic weights. By 1818 he had accurately calculated the atomic weights of 45 elements and suggested a new way of naming the elements by using the first letter or letters of their names, e.g. O = oxygen. Combinations of elements are represented by putting the letters together, e.g. CO_2 = carbon dioxide, one carbon atom joined to two oxygen atoms.

Atomic weight

Atoms are so small and light (there are approximately 602 billion trillion hydrogen ATOMS in a gram) that it is not strictly possible to weigh them. Therefore chemists use a RATIO of the average mass of the atoms of an ELEMENT instead of a very small unit. Carbon which has an atomic weight of 12, has been used as the reference point since 1961. An atomic weight is really the mass of an atom relative to that of one twelfth of a carbon atom. The term relative atomic mass is very often used as an alternative to atomic weight.

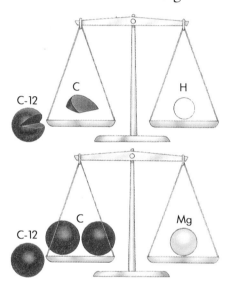

◀ *The reference element carbon has an atomic weight of 12. Hydrogen (H) is one twelfth the weight of a carbon-12 atom and so its atomic weight is one. Magnesium (Mg) is the weight of two carbon atoms and so its atomic weight is 24.*

▲ *The brilliant light displays of auroras are most common at the poles during intense sunspot activity.*

Aurora

Auroras are glows of light, hundreds of kilometres above the Earth's surface. They are seen when electrically-charged atomic particles, sprayed off the SUN's surface, collide with atoms in the Earth's atmosphere and make them release energy in the form of flashes of light.

The Sun sends out a steady stream of particles, but these do not normally cause auroras. However, once in a while a tremendous explosion, or *solar flare* occurs at a SUNSPOT. This sends a fountain of particles into space in a burst that usually lasts for just a few hours.

Electrically-charged particles are magnetic, and when they reach the magnetic field that surrounds the Earth some are pulled down towards the Earth's magnetic poles (close to the North and South poles). This is why auroras are strongest when observed from the arctic and antarctic.

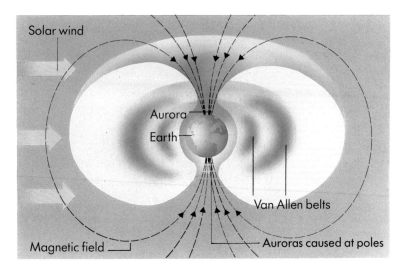

Solar wind
Aurora
Earth
Van Allen belts
Magnetic field
Auroras caused at poles

◄ Solar winds are streams of electrically-charged particles sprayed from the Sun. As they come near Earth some are trapped and pulled towards the poles by the Earth's magnetic field. Here they join particles in the Van Allen belts, two zones of electrically charged particles that surround the Earth. During intense sunspot activity the solar wind can disrupt the belts, striking particles and releasing energy in the form of light, creating auroras. The auroras in the Northern Hemisphere are called the aurora borealis and those in the Southern Hemisphere, aurora australis.

The most common colour in an aurora is green, but displays occurring very high in the sky may be shades of red or purple.

See also MAGNETISM; VAN ALLEN BELTS.

Automation

Automation is the use of machines to perform a wide variety of tasks. Automatic systems are especially useful for performing repetitive tasks. For example, robots are used on production lines to assemble car parts. Used in this way, machines can be extremely efficient since some tasks can be performed more cheaply by machines than by human workers. Electronic cash registers make an instant record of each item as it is sold and are able to place orders for new stock before an item runs out. Machines can also be used for decision making, for example, to regulate the flow of vehicles through sets of traffic lights.

▼ Some robots used in automation are very basic, like this mobot. It has flexible arms that are used for lifting and moving dangerous substances.

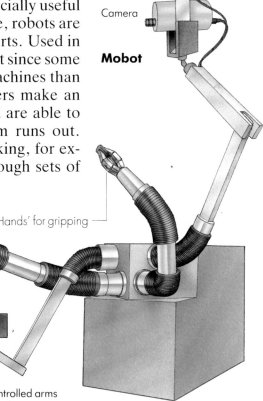

Camera

Mobot

'Hands' for gripping

Remote-controlled arms

An early example of automation was James Watt's flyball governor. Two balls were attached to a shaft that rotated at engine speed. When the engine speeded up, the balls were thrown further out. As they moved out, they controlled a steam inlet valve to the engine, allowing less steam in and slowing the engine.

► *Most robots are used in factories. They are often used for jobs such as welding, because they can be programmed to be very accurate.*

The earliest known example of automation is a water clock that is thought to have operated in Egypt in about 200 BC. The water clock consisted of a large tank full of water which was set up so water could flow out of a hole near the bottom of the tank and into a glass jar. On the jar was a scale marked off into the hours of the day. You could tell what time it was by looking at the level of water in the jar. As the level of water in the tank dropped, the water pressure decreased. You would normally expect the drop in water pressure to cause the water to flow more slowly into the jar, which would affect the accuracy of the clock. To prevent this, the drop in water level triggered a device that made the size of the hole in the tank larger to keep a constant flow of water into the jar.

An automatic system depends on information about the output and input of the system so it can regulate its performance. This is known as FEEDBACK. The system compares the actual output with the required output. If these are not the same, a device called a *controller* decides what to do to correct the error. The idea of a controller can be illustrated by thinking of a THERMOSTAT in a water heater. For example, say that the required temperature of the water is 65°C. The thermostat continually compares the temperature of the water as it heats up with the setting of 65°C on the thermostat. When the temperature of the water reaches the required point the thermostat switches the burner off. As the water starts to cool down the thermostat detects a fall in the temperature and switches the burner on again. In many systems COMPUTERS are used to control the various stages of an automated process.

Average Also called the arithmetic mean. The mean of a number of objects is like the idea of the balancing point, or centre of gravity.
Median The middle value in a group of numbers arranged in increasing order.
Mode The mode of a group of numbers is the number that occurs most frequently.

Average

The average of a set of quantities is the value that is most typical of that set. The value obtained by adding all the quantities in the set and dividing by the number of quantities is the *arithmetic mean*. For example, there are five children aged 13, 12, 10, 6 and 4. What is the average, or mean, of their ages? It is 9, 13+12+10+6+4=45 and 45 divided by 5 is 9. This is only one type of average. Others are also important, especially in STATISTICS. The *median* of a set of values is the middle value in the set. If our numbers, 13, 12, 10, 6 and 4, were marks out of 15 in a

Average height for the group (Mean)

test, the median would be the middle number 10. The *mode* is the number that appears most often in a set of numbers. Suppose ten children take a test. The marks they get out of 20 are: 18, 17, 15, 15, 13, 12, 12, 12, 9 and 6. The most frequent mark is 12, so 12 is the mode.

▲ To get the mean height of a group of people add all the heights together and divide the total by the number of people in the group.

SEE FOR YOURSELF
Fill some different shaped glasses with water. You can now work out the average amount of water contained in each glass. First pour the water from each of the glasses into a measuring jug. Next look to see how much water is in the jug. Do this by looking at the scale on the side of the jug. Then divide this figure by the number of glasses. You may need a calculator to do this. The resulting figure is the average.

Median height

▲ To find the median height of the group, arrange everybody in order of size. The median height is the height of the person in the middle.

Mode height

▲ The mode of the group is the most common height in the group.

Avogadro, Amedeo

Amedeo Avogadro (1776–1856) was an Italian physicist. He is famous for his gas law, known as Avogadro's law, which states that when each one of a set of identical glass jars is filled with a different GAS, at the same TEMPERATURE and PRESSURE, they each contain the same number of MOLECULES of gas. To discover the actual number of molecules requires the use of Avogadro's number. It is usually written as 6.0220×10^{23} which is a short way of writing 602,200,000,000,000,000,000,000. This is about the number of molecules of any gas, including AIR, that would be contained in 22.4 litres.

▼ Avogadro is known for his work in chemistry and physics.

▶ *Babbage worked on his second calculating machine, the Analytical Engine, from 1835 to 1848, but never finished it.*

▲ *Babbage spent much of his life developing two kinds of calculating machines.*

▼ *Baird is considered to be the 'father' of television.*

Babbage, Charles

Charles Babbage (1792–1871) resigned as Professor of Mathematics at Cambridge to work on designing a mechanical calculating machine. Despite the invention of logarithms, the need for accurate and complicated calculations had outgrown the existing simple machines, such as the ABACUS.

Babbage's aim was to use sets of GEARS that moved each other to produce columns of figures. These figures would then be printed out automatically.

His Difference Engine, as he called it, was never finished, but the beautifully-machined parts can be seen in the Science Museum, London. He abandoned it for the Analytical Engine, which was intended to solve algebraic problems as well as do direct calculations, but he could not find enough money to complete it. He is now respected as a computing pioneer born before his time.

Bacon, Roger *See* Alchemy

Baird, John Logie

Baird (1888–1946) was a Scottish engineer. In 1924 he became the first person ever to transmit a television picture by RADIO waves. He was also the first to transmit a picture across the Atlantic (in 1928), and in the same year he transmitted colour television pictures. Baird's first television apparatus, set up in his attic workshop at Hastings, England, included a tea chest, a biscuit tin, the front LENSES from a number of bicycle lamps, bits of wood, darning needles, string, and sealing-wax. This crude CAMERA transmitted a blurred image of a cross to a receiver at the other end of the attic.

Despite improvements made by Baird, in 1937 the British Broadcasting Corporation chose for its broadcasts a rival system that used a CATHODE RAY TUBE. *See also* ELECTROMAGNETIC RADIATION.

Balance *See* Scales and Balances

Balancing point

The balancing point of an object is the point at which it balances. The whole WEIGHT of the object appears to be concentrated in one spot. This point is called the CENTRE OF GRAVITY. If a regular-shaped object such as a tin can is tipped slightly it will fall back onto its base when released. If the can is tipped too far, beyond its balancing point, which is in the middle, this causes the can to become unstable and it will fall over.

Not all objects have their balancing point in the middle. An irregularly-shaped object such as a bus is designed to tilt over at a large angle without becoming unstable. This is done by making the chassis (the frame to which the engine and wheels are attached) of the bus very heavy which moves the balancing point, its centre of gravity, lower down. *See also* EQUILIBRIUM.

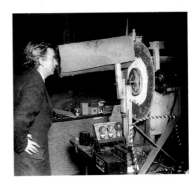

▲ *Baird first thought of sending pictures by radio waves in 1923. His mechanical scanning television system failed commercially, but he continued to experiment with picture transmission until his death.*

Baird kept improving his television system. Before World War II he gave a demonstration of TV in natural colours and just before he died it is said he had constructed a system for stereoscopic TV. He also invented an instrument called the 'Noctovision' for seeing in the dark.

If a person stands up in a rowing boat the balancing point is raised. Any slight disturbance is likely to cause the boat to tip over. The lifeboat has been designed with a low balancing point so that it can ride rough seas without being overturned. If it does happen to be overturned it will quickly right itself again.

SEE FOR YOURSELF
Tape a heavy weight into the corner of a box. Close the box, place it on a table and push it gently off the edge. You would normally expect an unweighted box, with its balancing point in the middle, to fall over the edge when it is about half-way off the edge of the table. By taping the weight in the corner of the box you have altered the weight and its even distribution throughout the box. This has moved the balancing point towards the corner. You can, therefore, push more than three-quarters of the box off the table before it falls over the edge.

Ballistics

Ballistics is a branch of engineering that studies the movement of bodies (called projectiles) which have been projected into the air. It is concerned mainly with: the path, or trajectory, of bullets fired from cannons and small arms; the free fall of bombs dropped from an aircraft; and the trajectory followed by a ROCKET or guided MISSILE once its engines have been turned off and it is acted upon only by the pull of gravity.

Interior ballistics investigates what happens to a bullet as it travels along a gun or rifle barrel, or a missile as it is fired from a launcher. *Exterior ballistics* examines the projectile in flight and its path to its target, and *terminal ballistics* studies how the projectile affects its target.

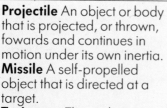

Projectile An object or body that is projected, or thrown, fowards and continues in motion under its own inertia.
Missile A self-propelled object that is directed at a target.
Trajectory The path an object follows as it moves through air under force.

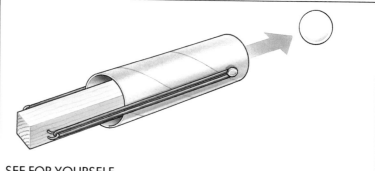

SEE FOR YOURSELF
Press 2 drawing pins through a kitchen roll tube into 2 very thin pieces of cork on the other side. Fix 2 elastic bands to 2 hooks on either side of a piece of wood that fits inside the tube. Hook the bands round the drawing pins. You can launch your ping-pong ball by pulling out the wood and letting it go.

▼ *In November 1783, a Montgolfier brothers' balloon made its first free flight with people on board. It took off from the centre of Paris, France.*

Balloon

Balloons are bags or sacks filled with a GAS. They are usually made from a non-porous material so the gas remains inside the balloon. If the balloon is filled with a gas which is lighter than AIR, such as HELIUM, the balloon will float upwards. In hot-air balloons, a gas burner is used to heat the air (hot air is lighter so the balloon rises). Balloons usually have a basket or other container attached to them to carry passengers. Ballooning is a popular pastime and sport.

Unmanned balloons are used for scientific research. Special balloons, carrying instruments, are sent into the upper ATMOSPHERE to measure and record information about temperature, wind, humidity and pressure.

To make your own hot air balloon you need sheets of tissue paper and glue.

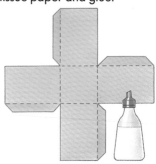

Cut the shape above out of paper, or glue 1 square and 4 rectangles of paper together.

Glue the long sides of the paper shape together to make it into a balloon.

Place a night light in a jar and light it carefully. Put the balloon over the jar and as the air heats up, the balloon will rise.

▲ As ballooning becomes a more popular sport, the colourful sight of the sky filled with hot air balloons is more common. Sometimes balloons are used to carry advertisements for particular products or services.

Bar code

A bar code is a series of black bars of different thicknesses with spaces between them. You will find bar codes printed onto the packaging of most goods that are bought in shops.

The width of the white spaces between the lines on a bar code is interpreted as a number by a scanner which is passed over the code. The number, which identifies the product, is then passed to a COMPUTER. In supermarkets and other large retail outlets low-powered LASER beam scanners are linked to a computerized till. The computer matches the current price of the item to the coded number and prints a description of the goods and its price onto the till receipt. With this system an accurate analysis of goods sold can be made and goods can be restocked before they sell out. Light pen scanners are used in some libraries to read the bar codes that are now being

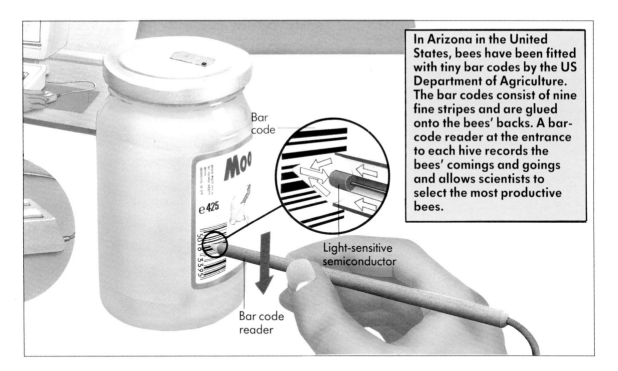

Bar code

Light-sensitive semiconductor

Bar code reader

In Arizona in the United States, bees have been fitted with tiny bar codes by the US Department of Agriculture. The bar codes consist of nine fine stripes and are glued onto the bees' backs. A bar-code reader at the entrance to each hive records the bees' comings and goings and allows scientists to select the most productive bees.

▲ Nowadays bar codes can be found on many products, since they provide an up-to-date record of stock in shops.

▼ It is difficult to see the intestine on an X-ray unless a 'barium meal' has been taken. A barium meal absorbs X-rays and so the intestine shows up clearly.

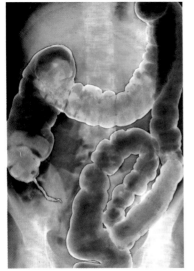

used to code books. The light pen sends the code to a computer which matches the book's unique number to the coded number of the borrower, recording which books are being taken out or returned. These systems can also issue reminder notices when borrowed books become overdue for return.

See also AUTOMATION; OPTICAL CHARACTER RECOGNITION.

Barium

Barium is a soft, heavy, silvery-white metallic element that readily reacts with other elements to form useful COMPOUNDS. Barium sulphate occurs in nature in the MINERAL barytes. Chemists make pure barium for laboratory work by passing an electric current through melted barium chloride. Barium compounds are used in paints, ceramics, special glass, liquid muds used in drilling oil wells, and for purifying chemical solutions and alloys.

Barium compounds that dissolve in water are poisonous, but barium sulphate, which is extremely insoluble, is harmless. When a doctor wishes to X-RAY a patient's digestive passage, the patient has to drink a barium 'meal' (a preparation of barium sulphate and water). The X-rays cannot pass through the barium sulphate, so when the photograph is developed, the intestines show up as a clear outline.

Barometer

A barometer measures changes in the PRESSURE of the ATMOSPHERE. This is the FORCE exerted on everything at the Earth's surface by the weight of the ATMOSPHERE. Changes in atmospheric pressure affect the WEATHER. By measuring these changes, barometers can be used to help forecast the weather.

Mercury barometers are used in weather stations. Atmospheric pressure on a reservoir of mercury causes the mercury to move up a long thin glass tube (with the air sucked out of it) until it cannot be pushed any higher. Usually this is when it is about 760 mm high. Variations in atmospheric pressure cause the liquid in the tube to rise or fall by small amounts which can be read off a scale. *See also* METEOROLOGY.

Evangelista Torricelli (1608–1647)
Torricelli was an Italian mathematician and physicist. He discovered the principle of the barometer. He put a long mercury-filled glass tube, closed at one end, upside-down in a cup of mercury. The air pressure on the surface of the mercury in the cup held the column of mercury in the tube at a height of 760 mm. The weight of the column of mercury was equal to the pressure of the atmosphere.

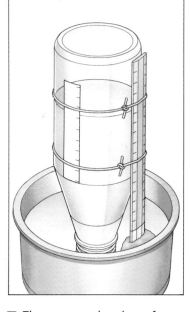

Mercury barometer

Column of mercury

Needle

Weights

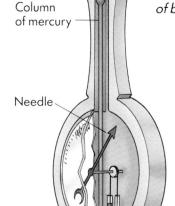

◄ Mercury barometers are the most sensitive and accurate type of barometer.

▼ The vacuum chamber of an aneroid barometer expands or contracts as the air pressure changes, causing the needle to move.

Aneroid barometer

Dial

Needle

Spindle

Lever

Vacuum chamber

▼ *The car battery* (right) *and the dry battery* (below) *are common kinds of battery. The car battery contains liquid acid, whereas the chemical in dry batteries is a paste. Another kind is the lithium battery used in calculators, watches, heart pacemakers and cameras.*

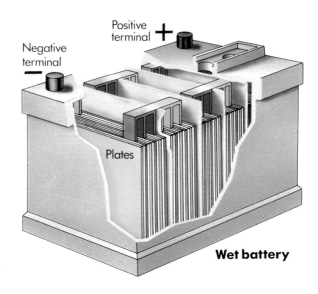

Negative terminal

Positive terminal

Plates

Wet battery

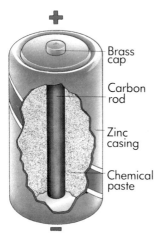

Brass cap

Carbon rod

Zinc casing

Chemical paste

Primary cells stop working once their chemical energy has been used up. They are then thrown away.
Secondary cells store electrical energy and can be recharged.

Another kind of dry cell has become more popular. This is the alkaline battery. It looks and acts much like the older type of torch battery but lasts considerably longer. Instead of ammonium chloride paste between the zinc case and the carbon rod it has a strong alkali solution called potassium hydroxide. This allows the cell to deliver high currents more efficiently than the ordinary zinc-carbon battery.

Battery

A battery uses chemicals to produce ELECTRICITY. There are two types: those that store or accumulate electricity (called accumulators) and can be recharged, and those that make electricity until their chemicals are exhausted.

The most common type of rechargeable battery is found in a car. Two metal plates, one of LEAD and the other of lead dioxide, are mounted inside a cell containing dilute SULPHURIC ACID. There are usually six cells, connected together, inside the battery case. The outer lead plate is connected to the negative terminal and the lead dioxide plate to the positive. The battery is first charged by connecting it to an ELECTRIC CIRCUIT. Then, after starting the ENGINE using the battery, a small dynamo turned by the engine keeps the battery charged up with electrical energy.

Torches use the second kind of battery, sometimes called a 'Leclanché dry cell'. It contains a paste of ammonium chloride inside a ZINC case, with a CARBON rod in the paste. The case makes the negative terminal and the rod, the positive one. Ammonium chloride is poisonous and so used batteries must be safely disposed of.

In many dry-cell batteries, the negative electrode is made of an amalgam of zinc, mercury and cadmium. This prolongs the life of the battery by reducing the rate at which the zinc dissolves in the battery liquids. Batteries turn chemical energy into electrical energy with an efficiency of about 90 percent. This is the most efficient but most expensive way of producing electricity.

Bearings

Bearings are devices in MACHINES that support moving parts and enable them to move with less FRICTION. The most common types are ball and roller bearings.

Almost every machine has bearings, for example, cars, bicycles, electric motors, ship's propellers and even roller skates. Where a shaft or rod passes through another part of a machine, such as an axle through the hub of a wheel, bearings are used to keep the two parts separated. Without bearings, the moving parts of the machine would constantly rub together and cause friction. Friction slows the machine down and also produces heat. It will eventually cause the parts to wear out.

A bearing is normally made up of an outer and inner ring of steel. The space between the rings contains either steel balls (known as ball bearings) or rollers (known as roller-contact bearings). These bearings slide or roll inside the rings.

After a great deal of use, it is usually only the bearings and not the machine that wear out.
See also ENERGY; LUBRICATION.

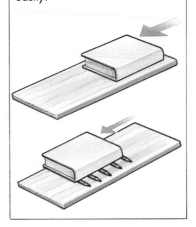

SEE FOR YOURSELF
Push a book along a wooden surface. Friction between the surface of the table and the book causes resistance and slows it down, increasing the amount of work you have to do. Now place 4 round pencils under the book. The pencils act like bearings. Friction is reduced and the book moves easily.

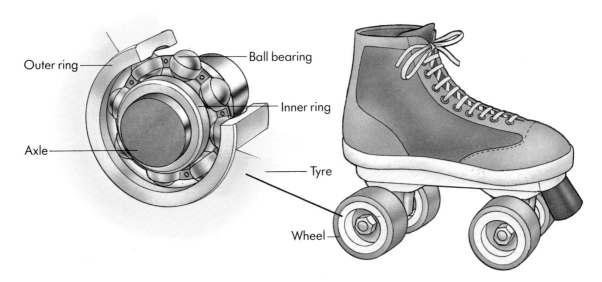

Outer ring — Ball bearing
Axle — Inner ring
Tyre
Wheel

▲ *Roller skate wheels contain ball bearings. These help the wheels move round smoothly, reducing friction and wear in the moving parts without the need for lubricants.*

Behaviour

Behaviour covers everything a human or other animal does during its life. Scientists who study behaviour are interested in finding out what affects behaviour. They want to know why an animal behaves in a certain way in a particular situation, for example, the way people

▲ In crowds people tend to copy one another, rather than act as individuals.

▼ Grebes have an elaborate courtship dance. The male crouches as he approaches the female, wings outstretched. Then a headwagging display begins. They often carry weeds in their beaks as they stretch their necks and sway. Finally the male will give the female a fish. This is instinctive behaviour.

behave in groups, how they sit or look at each other, or why some people shriek when they see a spider.

Behaviour has been divided into three main types: reflex, instinctive and learned behaviour. *Reflex actions* are not planned or decided beforehand. If you accidentally touch a hot object, you pull your hand away without thinking. *Instinctive behaviour* is behaviour that does not have to be learned. A young bird that has never seen another bird build a nest, does not have to be taught how to build one. Behaviour can be changed by LEARNING (*learned behaviour*). Many animals will run away when they hear a loud bang. But if the bangs are repeated often enough, the animal grows used to the noise and ceases to run away. It has changed its behaviour.

People's behaviour is more complicated than the behaviour of other animals. It is often difficult to separate instinctive behaviour from learned behaviour. For example, a person might inherit from his parents the capability to become a brilliant violinist, but without a violin and training he or she can never play the violin well.

See also GENETICS; PSYCHOLOGY AND PSYCHIATRY.

Bell, Alexander Graham

Alexander Graham Bell (1847–1922) was born and educated in Scotland but lived for most of his life in the United States of America. Before he left Scotland, Bell began teaching deaf children using a code of symbols invented by his father. His interest in the human voice, and the realization that speech produces SOUND waves vibrating in air, led him to become the first person to successfully transmit speech by means of electrified wire. In 1876, he announced the world's first workable TELEPHONE. It had certain disadvantages; it had to be moved quickly from mouth to ear and the sound was very faint even when the speaker shouted. The Amer-

▲ Alexander Bell, teacher of the deaf and inventor of the telephone.

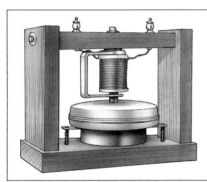

The First Bell Telephone
Alexander Graham Bell's telephone worked by changing sound produced by the human voice into electric current. This current could then be transmitted along a wire and changed back into sound at the other end. The telephone was invented while Bell and his assistant Watson were trying out a new transmitter for sending several telegraph messages at once. The first words were transmitted by accident. Watson heard Bell call from another room that he had spilt acid over his clothes.

ican inventor EDISON soon produced a much more powerful and successful telephone. In 1880, Bell brought out the *gramophone* which was an improved version of Edison's *phonograph*, a machine which recorded speech and played it back.

Though Bell will always be associated with the invention of the telephone, he would rather have been remembered as a teacher of the deaf.

Benzene

Benzene is a sweet-smelling, colourless LIQUID used for the industrial manufacture of several materials, such as polystyrene, synthetic rubber and nylon. It is also used in detergents and dyes. Benzene belongs to a class of chemicals called HYDROCARBONS. Each molecule of it contains six ATOMS of hydrogen and six atoms of carbon arranged in a ring formation. This is known as a benzene ring and is found in many other chemical compounds, including aspirin and the explosive TNT. Benzene is poisonous and can cause cancer. The British physicist

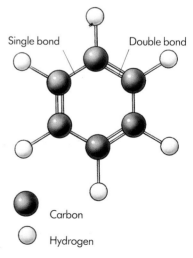

Single bond   Double bond

Carbon

Hydrogen

▲ The benzene ring consists of six atoms of carbon and six atoms of hydrogen.

August Kekulé, the German chemist, had a daydream in which he saw benzene atoms twisting and turning like snakes. One of the snakes seized its own tail. This gave Kekulé the idea that benzene is a ring of atoms.

Michael FARADAY discovered benzene in 1825. It was originally prepared by heating coal tar and changing its vapour into liquid. Large quantities of benzene are now extracted from PETROLEUM.

See also BOND, CHEMICAL; CHEMISTRY; PLASTICS.

Bessemer, Henry See Iron and Steel

Beta particles See Radioactivity

Big Bang theory

The Big Bang theory explains the origins of the UNIVERSE in terms of a 'big bang' that caused the GALAXIES to start moving apart at great speeds 15,000 million years ago. It must have been hotter and denser than we can imagine, a raging chaos of atomic particles. But physicists have calculated that in just *three minutes* these particles had turned into all the hydrogen ATOMS that now make up 90 percent of the Universe. As the hydrogen cloud expanded, it began to break up into separate clouds. These eventually became galaxies of stars like our own Milky Way galaxy, still moving apart from the Big Bang.

The Universe may expand for ever, or it may eventually stop expanding and then collapse inwards. But, it is predicted that before this, in about 5000 million years the Sun will expand, and burn the Earth.

See also COSMOLOGY; UNIVERSE.

▼ Some scientists believe that the Universe was created about 15,000 million years ago in an explosion called the Big Bang. Matter was formed in the tremendous heat that followed and galaxies were created.

Big Crunch theory

If all the GALAXIES in the UNIVERSE were stationary, their GRAVITY would attract each other and they would finally come together in a huge 'implosion'. The study of COS-MOLOGY shows that the galaxies are moving apart from the BIG BANG, but is their gravity strong enough to slow down their outward flight and eventually pull them back together?

The force of gravity of a body depends on its MASS. The galaxies do not contain enough mass to pull them back together, but there may be 'invisible' matter (single atoms) in the spaces between the galaxies. If this 'invisible' matter adds up to several times the material in the galaxies themselves, the extra gravity could reverse the expansion and event-ually cause a 'big crunch'.

▼ *The galaxies are still expanding, but the Big Crunch theory suggests that one day they will stop. Gravity will pull them together until they collide and implode.*

Implode To collapse violently inwards because of external pressure.
Explode To burst violently outwards as a result of internal pressure.

Some astronomers predict that in about 70 billion years time the galaxies will start moving together again. If this happens all the matter in the Universe will eventually come together in a big crunch. At this point there would be another big explosion, which would probably result in another Universe similar to the existing one.

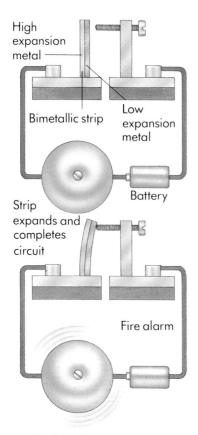

High expansion metal

Bimetallic strip

Low expansion metal

Battery

Strip expands and completes circuit

Fire alarm

▲ *This fire alarm system uses a bimetallic strip. When the strip heats up and bends, the electrical circuit is completed and the bell rings.*

▼ *The binary system is shown in cell division. Cells divide into two at each stage, until the egg is a mass of cells. This can be seen clearly in frog spawn with a magnifying glass.*

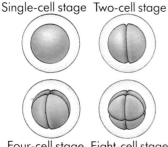

Single-cell stage   Two-cell stage

Four-cell stage   Eight-cell stage

Bimetallic strip

A bimetallic strip is made from pieces of two different metals stuck together along their length. When the strip is heated, each metal expands by different amounts. The strip forms a curve with the metal which expands more on the longer (outside) edge. The larger the temperature change the greater the amount of bending, so the strip is a sort of THERMOMETER.

It can be used in THERMOSTATS to help control TEMPERATURE. It is also used to turn on and off the flashing lamp of a car indicator. The electric current lights the lamp and also heats a bimetallic strip, which bends away from the contact and breaks the electrical circuit. This turns off the lamp and stops the heating, the strip cools and straightens, re-makes the circuit and turns the lamp on again.

See also ELECTRICITY; EXPANSION.

Binary numbers

The binary number system uses only two digits: 0 and 1. With a binary number the digit on the right has the value one, the next digit going left is two times larger and the next is two times larger again. So, reading from right to left, the first place has a value of 1, the second of 2, the

Binary numbers   Decimal numbers

64	32	16	8	4	2	1		100	10	1
----	----	----	----	----	----	----		-----	----	---
0	1	0	0	1	0	1			3	7
1	1	0	1	1	1	0		1	1	0
0	1	1	0	1	0	1				

◄ *Can you work out what this binary number is as a decimal number? Answer on page 65.*

third of 4, the fourth of 8, the fifth place of 16 and so on, doubling each time. Following this system, the binary number 101 means one 4, no 2s and one 1 which when added together is 5 in the DECIMAL system. In COMPUTERS binary numbers are used to code information by setting the many tiny electrical switches either to on or to off.

See also MATHEMATICS; NUMBERS.

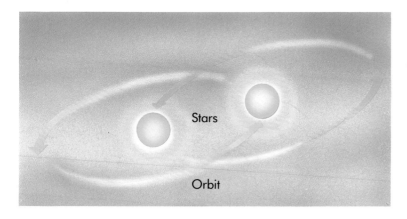

Stars

Orbit

◀ Binary stars are pairs of stars which are born together. The force of gravity holds them close so that they orbit around each other. Binary stars are often different in shape and brightness.

Binary stars

Binary stars, sometimes known as double stars, are pairs of stars that revolve around each other and are held together by GRAVITY. The closer a pair of stars are, the faster they revolve. Some binary stars are almost touching, and go around each other in a few hours. Others are separated by hundreds of times the diameter of the SOLAR SYSTEM and may take a million years to orbit each other. About a quarter of all the stars in our Milky Way GALAXY have at least one companion in space. The star *Castor* in the constellation *Gemini* is really six stars!

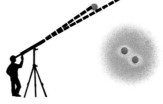

▲ When viewed through a telescope a pair of stars may appear close together, although one may be many thousands of kilometres in front of the other. These are called optical double stars.

Binimage

Binocular vision is the type of vision many animals have, in which each EYE sees a single object from a slightly different direction. If you move your head from side to side an object will appear to move slightly against other objects in the background. This is called PARALLAX and

▶ Animals can judge distances better if their eyes are in front, because they have a larger area of binocular vision.

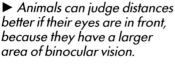

Owl

Human

Hare

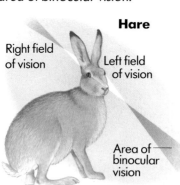

Right field of vision

Left field of vision

Area of binocular vision

◀ Animals with eyes at the side of their heads can see all the way round, although they only have a small area of binocular vision.

▶ In this breathing experiment, biochemists are able to examine the chemical changes that take place during respiration.

Antoine Lavoisier and the Marquis de Laplace were among the first scientists to carry out experiments in biochemistry. They demonstrated that animal respiration was chemically similar to combustion (burning). Lavoisier also demonstrated that food gives the body energy.

it helps animals to judge how far away an object is. Some animals with binocular vision, including humans, have eyes on the front of their heads giving them *stereoscopic vision*. The brain builds up a three-dimensional picture from the two eyes, enabling the animal to judge distance and depth accurately. The amount the eyes have to FOCUS on an object tells the brain how far away it is.

Biochemistry

The science of biochemistry, in which the methods of the chemist are used to find out about biological processes going on in living things, is a very complex and very important one. All plants and animals are made up of chemical COMPOUNDS and it is the task of the biochemist to discover the structure of these substances and work out what part they play in keeping the plant or animal alive. Carbohydrates, proteins, lipids (fats and oils), and nucleic acids such as DNA, which are all essential for cell building, are just some of the chemical molecules that are subjects of study by biochemists. They have used their knowledge in medicine, where GENETIC ENGINEERING is used to make vaccines against VIRAL DISEASES such as mumps. Biochemists are also working to find cures for such DISEASES as CANCER and AIDS.

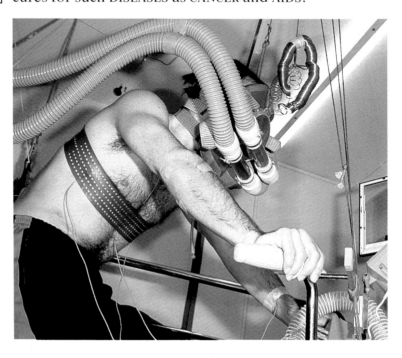

Biodegradable *See* Pollution

Biological control

Biological control is the system of killing pests with their natural enemies instead of with poisonous PESTICIDES. It is less damaging than spraying poison everywhere, as long as these enemies will not attack other organisms when they have got rid of the pests. Insects, fungi and

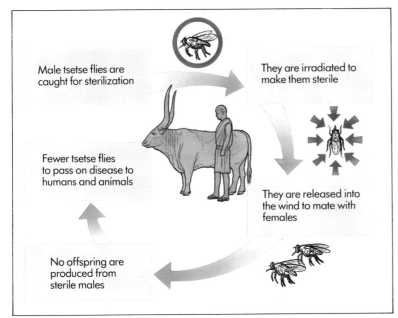

Male tsetse flies are caught for sterilization

They are irradiated to make them sterile

Fewer tsetse flies to pass on disease to humans and animals

They are released into the wind to mate with females

No offspring are produced from sterile males

several larger animals have all been used to control pests. A small American moth successfully controlled the prickly pear cactus, which spread rapidly through Australia after being introduced from the United States. On the other hand, large toads were introduced from Hawaii to try and control the sugar cane beetle in Australia. They did not eat the beetles, they ate lots of other animals and many birds died when they tried to eat the poisonous toads. The toads have now become serious pests and the cane beetle still damages the sugar cane.

Biology

Biology is the study of living things. It is one of the three major divisions of science, with PHYSICS and CHEMISTRY. There are about two million known living species, and it is clearly impossible for a biologist to study them all. For this reason, biology is subdivided into several more specialized sciences each concerned with a particular form of life or activity. *See* pages 66 and 67.

▲ *Tsetse flies like this are the cause of many problems in Africa, because they carry parasites and spread disease.*

Answer to Binary question on page 62:
110101 is 53—one 32, one 16, one 4 and one 1 added together to give 53.

◄ *Various attempts have been made to control tsetse flies. The method shown here uses radiation to sterilize males.*

BIOLOGY

The word biology is derived from Greek and means 'knowledge of life' Originally, biologists studied the structure or anatomy of animals and plants, and tried to describe their relationships with each other. It was soon realized that some types of living organisms were closely related and could be grouped into families. Study of the anatomy of animals and humans led quickly to the development of surgery and to medicine becoming a science in its own right.

Specialized biologists are now more interested in how living organisms work and behave. Some of the most important work in biology is directed towards finding out how cells work. This type of study could lead to prevention or cure of many diseases. Biologists have learned how to manipulate and alter the genes inside the cell. The genes control how an organism lives and grows.

The study of genetics has enabled the development of new types of cultivated plants, which are healthier and produce larger crops than the original types. Similarly, farm animals are bred to grow faster and reach a larger size, or produce more milk or wool.

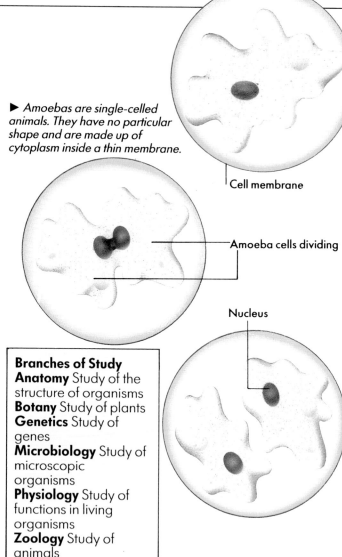

▶ Amoebas are single-celled animals. They have no particular shape and are made up of cytoplasm inside a thin membrane.

Cell membrane

Amoeba cells dividing

Nucleus

Branches of Study
Anatomy Study of the structure of organisms
Botany Study of plants
Genetics Study of genes
Microbiology Study of microscopic organisms
Physiology Study of functions in living organisms
Zoology Study of animals

▲ Biologists study the growth of plants in plant breeding experiments. Plant tissue such as this can be grown from a single plant cell in a special mixture containing salts, vitamins and growth substances.

SEE FOR YOURSELF
You need a narrow wooden-framed box with 2 glass sides. Make airholes in the top. Three-quarters fill the box with several layers of different types of soils. Put leaves on the surface and add 3 or 4 earthworms. After a few days, the different layers of soil become mixed as the worms burrow up and down through them. The leaves will be pulled down and eaten.

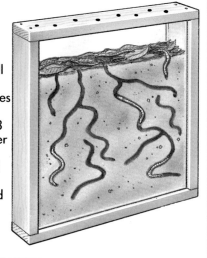

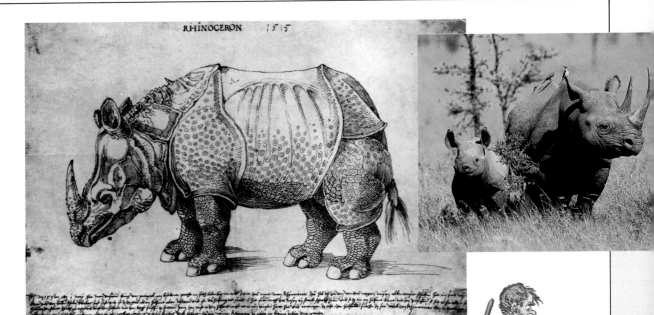

RHINOCERON 1515

▲ *Compare the photograph of the rhinoceroses with this drawing made by Durer who had never seen a rhinoceros.*

Milestones in Biology
1000 BC Ancient Egyptians study human anatomy.
1300–1600 The importance of experimentation and observation is realized.
1735 Linnaeus classifies animals according to structural similarities. System still used today.
1800s Schlieden and Schwann show that the cell is the basic unit of life.
1859 Darwin publishes *On the Origin of Species*, which describes the theory of evolution and the principle of natural selection.
1953 Watson and Crick propose DNA structure.
1970s Biologists discover genetic engineering.

▶ *When cowpox was used as a vaccination for smallpox in 1796, some people thought they would turn into cows. This cartoon by Cruikshank makes fun of such an idea.*

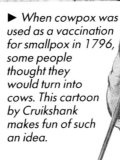

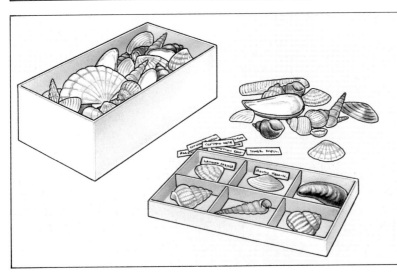

SEE FOR YOURSELF
Collect and classify different types of shells. Try to find out the name of each one. You can do this by looking in a book about shell identification, which you should be able to find in your local library. Make a box with separate compartments in it. Choose the best example of each shell type, put it into a compartment and label it with its name.

See also ANATOMY; BIOCHEMISTRY; BIOPHYSICS; BIOTECHNOLOGY; BOTANY; GENETICS; MEDICINE; PHYSIOLOGY; ZOOLOGY.

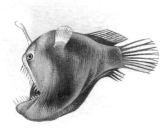

▲ *Deep within the ocean, where sunlight cannot reach, fish such as the angler fish use bioluminescence to find food or to attract a mate.*

Bioluminescence

Bioluminescence is the production of light by living organisms, such as fireflies, glowworms, and many animals that live in the sea. The lights are produced by CHEMICAL REACTIONS in various parts of the animals' body. In these reactions, OXYGEN is combined with a substance called luciferin, and ENERGY is given out in the form of light. Unlike our electric lights, the lights give out almost no heat. The animals turn their lights on and off by altering the amount of oxygen reaching them. Some fungi and bacteria produce glowing light, but it is not yet clear how.

Fireflies (a kind of beetle) are found in many parts of the world. Some flash while resting on trees or on the ground, and others, while flying. The lights bring the males and females together for mating. Many deep-sea fish produce light to find their way or to attract prey.

▶ *Sometimes the sea appears to be lit by a strange light. The light actually comes from luminescent organisms including certain bacteria and fungi. Many squids are also luminescent. The light comes from the chemical processes that go on in the cells of these plants and animals.*

The chemical process used by animals to produce bioluminescence has been copied by scientists to produce cold lights that are used for emergency lighting and also in the glowing bracelets and necklaces that are often sold in fairgrounds. These lights glow brightly until the light-producing chemicals inside them are used up.

Biophysics

Biophysics is a mixture of BIOLOGY and PHYSICS, in which scientists use the methods of the physicists to investigate living things. Biophysics is particularly important in investigating the way the human body works. The motion of the BLOOD being pumped around the body, the action of the HEART and other MUSCLES, and blood pressure are all processes and activities that can be explained by means of physics. The physical process of DIFFUSION, for example, is used to explain the exchange of gases between the blood and cells and the blood and the lungs.

◀ *Biophysics has taught us much about the function of the human body. Research into muscle movements has helped in the development of artificial limbs.*

An important area of biophysics is the detailed study of the structure of molecules in living things. One of the best known achievements in the field of biophysics was in 1953 when Crick and Watson constructed a model of the DNA (deoxyribonucleic acid) molecule. DNA is the hereditary material of life. The cells of organisms contain DNA strands grouped together in chromosomes. The combination of DNA molecules determines the shape and form of offspring.

The effects of physical stimuli on living organisms, such as LIGHT, SOUND, PRESSURE and external force, are also examined by biophysicists.
See also MOVEMENT AND MOTION.

Biotechnology

Biotechnology is the use of organisms to make or change products. Its use dates from the first fermented drinks, such as beer, made by people thousands of years ago.

Microscopically small organisms such as bacteria can process some materials more efficiently than normal industrial methods. Some fuels can be made by bacteria. For example, bacteria feeding on household waste produce a gas called METHANE. Methane burns easily and so it can be used as a fuel. At least five species of bacteria

SEE FOR YOURSELF
Add 2 tablespoons of live yoghurt to a pint of milk and gently heat them together. This process causes the milk to ferment. The bacteria in the yoghurt turns the lactose (milk sugar) in the milk into lactic acid, which makes the milk thicken. The result is yoghurt.

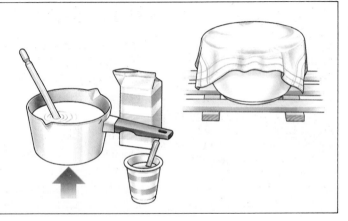

One of the first examples of biotechnology can be traced back to 1916. A liquid called acetone (now also known as propanone) was needed to make explosives during the World War I. The British Admiralty Powder Department found that it was possible to ferment grain by special bacteria called *Clostridium acetobutylicum*, which enabled it to be converted into several substances, including acetone.

make cold water form ice crystals. This is being used to develop a quick test to identify food infected by Salmonella, the bacteria which causes FOOD POISONING. The ice-producing part of a bacteria is transferred into a VIRUS that attacks Salmonella. If ice forms when food is chilled this means the virus is inside Salmonella. Similar tests for other food-spoiling bacteria are being developed. In the 1970s, the new field of GENETIC ENGINEERING provided scientists with a way of altering genetic material (the living material inside every cell of the body that controls GROWTH and development).

See also FERMENTATION; GENETICS; MICROORGANISMS.

Birth

Birth is the series of events that carry a baby from inside its mother's body to the outside world. A baby mammal develops in a muscular bag called the womb inside its mother's body. Birth begins when HORMONES in the mother's blood tell the muscles of the womb to start to contract and push the baby towards the womb's opening. In humans, we call this process labour, probably because it is hard work for the mother. As the contractions become stronger, the baby's head bursts the bag of fluid that protected it while it was inside its mother, and further contractions push the baby right out of the mother's body.

Birth occurs in egg-laying animals when the offspring emerge (hatch) from the egg to begin life independently from their parents.

See also EMBRYO; REPRODUCTION.

▼ The female kangaroo gives birth to a tiny baby (a joey), which develops in its mother's pouch. There, the joey attaches itself to a teat and feeds on its mother's milk for several months.

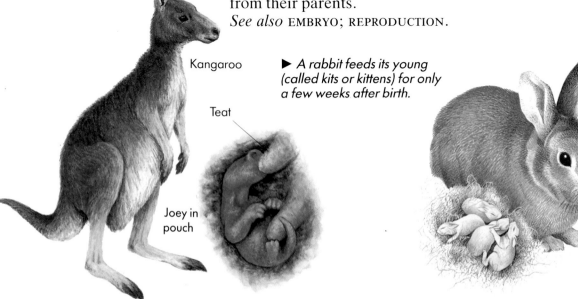

Kangaroo

Teat

▶ A rabbit feeds its young (called kits or kittens) for only a few weeks after birth.

Joey in pouch

Bit and Byte

A bit is the smallest piece of information that a COMPUTER can process and a byte is a group of eight bits operating together as a single unit.

The word bit is formed from 'binary digit'. A bit can only have one of two values, zero or one. Every character (letter, number or symbol) on a computer keyboard can be represented by a group of eight bits, a byte. For example, the letter A is represented by 01000001 and the number 8 by 00111000. Every character typed on a computer, or sent to another device such as a printer is represented in this way according to a standard code called American Standard Code for Information Interchange, or ASCII (pronounced askey).

> A **byte** is a space in the computer's memory that is occupied by one character. A group of four bits, or half a byte, is called a **nibble**.

Bitumen

Bitumen is a thick, sticky liquid or solid. It is brownish or black in colour, consisting of HYDROCARBONS and the substances derived from them. There are various types of bitumen. Many types burn easily and are valuable as fuels. Some bitumen is produced by the DISTILLATION of crude oil. We also get it from naturally-occurring MINERALS, such as bituminous (soft) coal, tar, asphalt, PETROLEUM and naphtha. Bituminous sands, a major source of crude oil, contain up to 13 percent of bitumen. Bitumen is used in making oil, waterproof coating, electrical insulation and in road building.

▲ The surface of a road is coated with asphalt, a type of bitumen which wears well, is weatherproof and is unharmed by most salts and acids.

Parrot

Chick hatching from egg

Male seahorse

Young

Pouch

▶ The female seahorse lays its eggs in the male's pouch. They are released when they have developed. After a day the young can look after themselves.

◀ A young bird is born as an egg, which hatches after a few weeks. The mother feeds it until it can fly and feed itself.

71

Black body

The term 'black body' means an object that absorbs all ELECTROMAGNETIC RADIATION that falls on it and does not radiate any. No perfect black body really exists. If a dull black surface is illuminated with light, almost all the light will be absorbed. In fact, it is because no light is reflected to our eyes that the surface appears black. A surface covered with pure carbon will absorb about 97 per cent of all light striking it.

Black hole

Space is not empty because it is invisible. Beams of light do not pass through it in straight lines, because GRAVITY can 'bend' space so that light, or anything else (such as a spacecraft) passing through it, travels in a curve. Even around our huge and massive SUN, space is only curved by a small amount. But the force of gravity around a

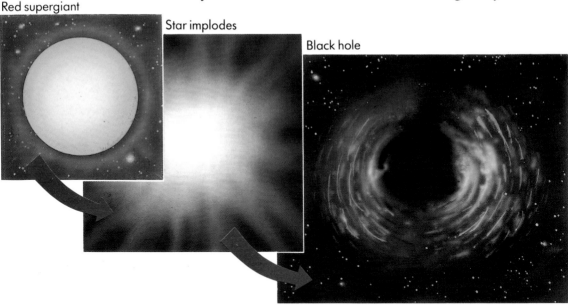

Red supergiant

Star implodes

Black hole

Distorted light from distant stars behind the black hole

▲ *Black holes are thought to be the final stage in a large star's life. The star collapses inwards in a huge implosion, leaving a 'hole'. It is seen as a hole because there is such a strong gravitational pull, no light can escape from the star.*

very large star that has collapsed can be so strong that the nearby space is curved into a complete circle. The light sent out from the star cannot escape into space so the star cannot be seen. It is a black hole.

Black holes can be detected. Single stars which behave like a member of a BINARY STAR system may have black holes as invisible companions, for example, the X-ray source, Cygnus X-1. There are probably millions of black holes in the MILKY WAY alone.

forces. He has shown that they give off particles and radiation until they explode and disappear. Hawking is generally thought to have made some of the most important finds about gravity since Einstein's theory of general relativity. He is currently working on combining gravity and a branch of physics known as quantum mechanics in a single theory that can explain the origin and structure of the Universe. He holds the post of Lucasian professor of physics at Cambridge University, a post Sir Isaac Newton once held. Hawking has suffered from an incurable disease of the nervous system since the 1960s.

Stephen Hawking (1942–)
Hawking is a British theoretical physicist. He is best known for his theories about black holes, which are invisible bodies in space with strong gravitational

The size of a star decreases greatly when it becomes a black hole. If the Sun, which is a star, was to become a black hole, its existing diameter of 1,392,000 km would have to be compressed into a diameter of just 6 km. The idea of the black hole was first developed by the German astronomer Karl Schwarzschild in 1916.

Blast furnace

A blast furnace is a very important part of the IRON AND STEEL industry. Rock called ORE, rich in iron oxide, is loaded into the blast furnace together with measured amounts of coke (a kind of processed COAL) and limestone that helps to remove some of the impurities from

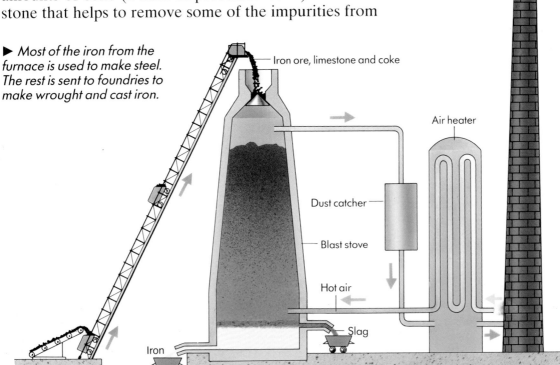

▶ Most of the iron from the furnace is used to make steel. The rest is sent to foundries to make wrought and cast iron.

Waste gases

Iron ore, limestone and coke

Air heater

Dust catcher

Blast stove

Hot air

Slag

Iron

▲ *To melt iron temperatures above 1600°C are needed. Blast furnaces are lined with firebrick that can withstand extremely high temperatures. When the lining wears out, the furnace must be shut down so that the lining can be replaced. The lining can last up to three years with 7000 tonnes of iron and steel being processed each day.*

the molten iron. Inside the furnace hot, dry air, at high PRESSURE, is blasted in through the bottom causing the coke to burn. This raises the temperature towards the bottom of the furnace to a point where the OXYGEN in the iron oxide reacts with CARBON MONOXIDE from the coke and the iron melts. Every three or four hours the molten iron is run off. The impurities (known as slag) floating on the surface of the iron are removed and the molten iron then flows into moulds to form large bars of 'pig' iron that can be processed to make steel.

Bleaching

Bleaching is the process of removing the colour from something. Sunlight is a very good bleach. This was a fact well known to the ancient Egyptians, who brightened and whitened their cloth by exposing it to the sun. We still bleach textiles today, to prepare them for dyeing or to remove a DYE from them. Industrial bleaching is a chemical process using a bleach based on SODIUM chlorate. This compound breaks down in use to release OXYGEN, which is a very good bleaching agent. Almost all flour for baking used to be bleached, but now unbleached flour is available. In the home, bleaches are used for cleaning and brightening clothes and also as a disinfectant.

In the 17th century in Europe, oil of vitriol (sulphuric acid) was used to bleach the hair. It is now more sensibly used in car batteries. Today hydrogen peroxide is the main ingredient in products made for bleaching hair. It is also widely used to bleach cotton cloth.

Safety with Bleach
Always handle bleach with great care. Bleach contains dangerous chemicals, which can be harmful to health if swallowed. Make sure you wear rubber gloves to protect your skin and, if necessary, safety goggles to protect your eyes. Wipe up any spillages immediately.

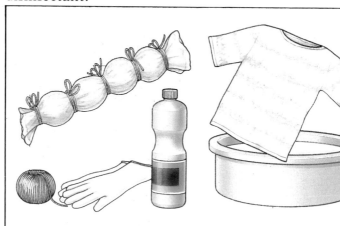

SEE FOR YOURSELF
Take an old coloured T-shirt, roll it up and tie it tightly with string in about 4 or 5 places. Add a solution of bleach to a bowl of water. Put the T-shirt into the bowl and leave for 30 minutes.

Take it out of the solution and rinse it in cold water. Untie the strings and rinse again. The bleach has removed the colour from the parts of the T-shirt not covered by strings.

BLOOD

Blood is the vital life-sustaining liquid that is found in the bodies of all large animals. It is pumped round the body by the heart through an network of arteries, veins and capillaries. The kidneys control the amount of water in the blood and expel, as urine, the waste products of the body. The blood carries oxygen, and food materials from the digestive system to the body tissues.

In humans about 20 percent of body weight is blood and other fluids not included in the body cells. The basis of blood is a straw-coloured liquid called plasma, in which the food materials, waste products, hormones etc. are dissolved. Plasma can pass through the cell walls. It has millions of blood cells floating in it which have two main functions: carrying oxygen and fighting disease. In vertebrates, blood is red because of flat disc-shaped red cells or erythrocytes. These contain hemoglobin, which absorbs oxygen in the lungs, and releases it in the tissues. The disease-fighting cells are known as white cells or leucocytes. Some attack invading organisms and clear away dead cells, others produce anti-bodies that kill the germs and destroy their poisons. Blood platelets are very small cells which make the blood clot.

In humans, everyone belongs to one of four blood groups (A, B, O and AB). The letters indicate the presence or absence of particular substances in the blood. Some blood groups cannot be mixed, if they are the blood sticks together.

◀ This test tube shows the parts of blood after they have been separated in a centrifuge.
Plasma

White blood cells and platelets

Red blood cells

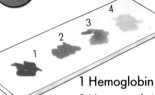

1 Hemoglobin
2 Hemoerythrin
3 Hemocyanin
4 Chlorocruorin

▲ Animal blood is not always red. Different blood pigments have different colours. Hemoglobin is the most common. Hemocyanin is bluish and is found in some invertebrates.

◀ The three types of blood cells found in human blood. Red blood cells are doughnut-shaped, white blood cells are round and platelets are disc-shaped. Anemia is a condition in which the number of red blood cells falls below normal. The shortage of oxygen causes tiredness and weakness.

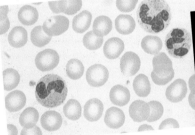 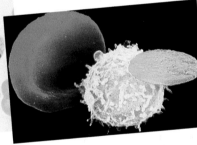

▲ White blood cells have a nucleus, unlike red blood cells. Here, the nucleus of the white blood cells has been stained purple.

▼ During a blood transfusion a patient must be given a compatible blood group. This table shows which blood groups can be mixed.

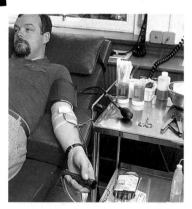

	Blood group	Antigens on red cells	Antibodies in plasma	Can receive blood type
	A	A	B	A and O
	B	B	A	B and O
Universal recipient	AB	A and B	none	A, B, AB, O
Universal donor	O	none	A and B	O

▲ Donated blood is stored in blood banks for use in transfusions.

See also AIDS; ANTIBODIES AND ANTIGENS; CIRCULATION; HEART; OXYGEN.

▲ Doctors analyse pictures of organs in a patient's body using the computerized tomography system.

Body scanner

A body scanner is a machine used in MEDICINE to produce pictures of the inside of the body. There are two basic types of scanner. The first uses a process called computerized tomography (CT). A thin beam of X-RAYS is fired through the body at different angles. The results registered by X-ray detectors are analysed by a COMPUTER which adds up all the individual results to make a picture of a slice through the body. The second type of scanner uses a process called magnetic resonance (MR). Hydrogen particles in the body move a minute amount in a magnetic field and then give out a field of their own. This can be detected by sensors in the MR scanner and, as in a CT scanner, analysed by computer to produce a picture of a slice through the body.

Bohr, Niels *See* Atom

Boiling point

The boiling point of a substance is the TEMPERATURE at which it changes from a LIQUID to a GAS or VAPOUR. Boiling occurs because the MOLECULES which make up the liquid move around more quickly as the temperature rises, until they escape from the liquid into the gas. Lighter molecules move around faster than heavier ones and some sorts of molecules stick together in liquid more strongly than others. This means that the boiling points of different substances can be very different.
See also EVAPORATION; FREEZING POINT; MELTING POINT.

▲ When a pan of water boils water vapour is released. The water vapour is only visible when it condenses and then it is called steam.

▶ The boiling point of a liquid depends on air pressure. Air pressure decreases with altitude so water, which normally boils at 100°C, boils at 72°C at 3048 m above sea level.

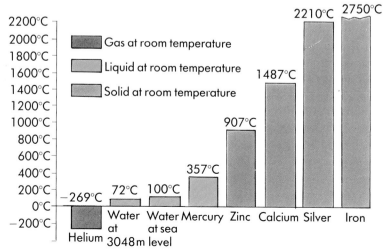